WOMEN
NOVELISTS
TODAY

WOMEN NOVELISTS TODAY

A SURVEY OF ENGLISH WRITING IN THE SEVENTIES AND EIGHTIES

Olga Kenyon

Head of Humanities, Morley College

THE HARVESTER PRESS

First published in 1988 by
The Harvester Press Ltd,
16 Ship Street, Brighton, Sussex
A Division of
Simon & Schuster International Group
© Olga Kenyon, 1988

Printed and bound in Great Britain by
Biddles Ltd, Guildford and King's Lynn

British Library Cataloguing in Publication Data

Kenyon, Olga
Women novelists today: a survey of English writing
in the seventies and eighties.
1. English fiction — Women authors —
History and criticism 2. English fiction
— 20th century — History and criticism
I. Title
823'. 914'099287   PR888.W6
ISBN 0–7108–0964–6
ISBN 0–7108–1162–4 Pbk

2   3   4   5   92 91 90 89 88

Contents

Acknowledgements

I should like to thank these friends and colleagues for their help and encouragement: Jennifer Bailey, Christopher Branson, Margaret Chalker, Dr Peter Conradi, Geoff Diggines, Celia Gibbs, David Kenyon, Ian Le Maistre, David Mitchell and Dr Winifred Stevenson.

Preface

A special feature of this study is the inclusion of comments from interviews given to me by these novelists. I should like to thank them for the generosity with which they gave their time and opinions. All these writers are illuminating critics as well as fabulators, and their views enrich this book. The diversity of their artifice bears witness to the ebullience of the 'female imagination'. We are fortunate to live in an era of marked originality in fiction and criticism. Women's writing and feminist criticism have experienced a rebirth in the 1970s and 1980s. And it is literature, especially the novel, to which criticism, psychoanalysis and sociology have gone for their images of women. The novel is the most sensitive register of our experience today. It explores the world as it is said to be and as we experience it. No other literary form is so capacious, so concerned with the whole human being, alone and in society, without limitation of specialist viewpoints. A study of women novelists charts the consciousness of our time.

'I look to a future where gender no longer divides us.'

'Vive la différence!'

Introduction

The 1970s and 1980s display increasing diversity and force in women's writing. Women are once again shaping the novel, as in the eighteenth century, when they mothered realism, romance and the gothic. In the last two decades they have extended the main modes of narration, from the conventional to the fantastic. In the 1960s women in Britain revived the dulled realist novel with their (often) anguished attempts to identify and express their situation. Now they are exuberantly adapting fantasy, from science fiction to magazine fiction, in order to explore the limits imposed on our conscious and unconscious minds.

Women novelists in Britain have an unusually rich tradition of women writers to give them confidence in the use of a variety of forms. Jane Austen introduced fine comedy into her moralising social stories. The Brontës transformed the gothic with dream and female indignation. George Eliot extended realism to include the intellectual life of her time. Virginia Woolf embraced impressionism and experimented with structure. Such models were almost taken away from women to be subsumed into the 'malestream' of the novel, but are now being reclaimed to demonstrate women's range and versatility.

WHY THE WRITERS IN THIS STUDY HAVE BEEN SELECTED

The writers in this study have been chosen as each represents a vitally different attitude to the potential of fiction. Iris

Murdoch is a major moral thinker, using the novel in the two main ways initiated by eighteenth-century women: as realistic study of human beings and as artfully contrived fabulation. Antonia Byatt combines nineteenth-century realism and twentieth-century questioning of language to create novels of remarkable intelligence, some of the most interesting writing in England today. Margaret Drabble examines the restrictions felt by young mothers, in conventional forms, giving them new validity. Eva Figes adapts the flow of impressionism to explore female sensations, from birth to old age. Fay Weldon innovates with the punchy paragraphs of copy-writing to mock conventional attitudes to femininity, and suggests ways of escape. Anita Brookner revindicates the 'women's' novel to represent the limitations still felt by women.

The ideological differences between these writers is vast and fascinating. Ideology means (since Althusser) the sum of ways in which people both live and represent their relationship to their conditions of existence. Ideology is inscribed, often unconsciously, in discourses, myths, presentations of 'how things are'. It is not free-floating but embodied in words, in thinking and experiencing – the realm of the novel.

Iris Murdoch accepts patriarchy in that she does not feel excluded from the discourse of philosophy, indeed feels free to enter the male psyche as narrator. 'Patriarchy' is a controversial term but useful to describe a society dominated by white, middle-class males – in Parliament, the law, the media, the Church – who frequently exclude other groups, either consciously or unconsciously.[1] Antonia Byatt posits a creative mind which is androgynous, sharing male and female attributes. Like George Eliot she represents men with almost as much skill as women; and both explore problems in science, resisting exclusion. They and Margaret Drabble continue to vindicate the realist novel, based on the assumption that it reflects the reality of experience as it is perceived by one individual who expresses it in a discourse which enables other individuals to recognise it as true. However she implicitly attacks the exclusiveness of patriarchal language by using gynaecological terms to overcome shame and concealment.

Eva Figes rejects patriarchal discourse, even traditional novel form, to foreground female consciousness. Fay Weldon refuses conventional stereotypes for women by making childrearing and sexuality the areas for combatting patriarchy.

THE EFFECT OF WOMEN'S LIBERATION

Most of these novelists began writing (though Iris Murdoch began earlier) in the 1960s when women's concerns gained adherents. They were consecrated in the 1970s when the women's liberation movement took a quantum leap forward. The focus on the types of life women lead soon produced a politicising of issues raised in 1960s books; why women felt dissatisfied with the roles assigned to them in patriarchy; why mothers suffered the physical intransigence of their homes – or the strain of two jobs; why did society suggest women could be freer yet load them with guilt?; how far we are influenced (or not) by biology; how to combat restrictive male images.

There were many different reactions from socialist feminists who believed that socialism could be adapted to include the concerns of women, to radical feminists who posit a social organisation in which men have power over women and must thus be opposed. There has been a valuable cross-fertilisation between feminism and the novel. Feminists have gone to literature to examine (and deconstruct) restrictive images which males have created of females. Feminism has aided novelists by privileging women's experience and by encouraging women's presses. The main growth area in publishing now is books on, for and by women, read by an increasing female readership. Virago proved that women want to read more than male publishers were offering them. It is significant that the one novelist in this study to be acclaimed before Women's Lib was Iris Murdoch, who often makes men her protagonists.

Since the eighteenth century the majority of novel readers have been women, a witness to their powers of imagination, their interest in analysis of relationships. Yet women writers are still marginalised by many reviewers under the pejorative heading of 'women'. Male writers from Connolly to Mailer wilfully, publicly, underestimate female qualities. Nadine Gordimer and Doris Lessing have a greater claim to the Nobel Prize than many men. Universities feature remarkably few women writers on their courses, and have fought the introduction of women's studies. Examination boards are the worst, continuing perpetrators of neglect, choosing *still* only 8 per cent of books by women to 92 per cent of male writers.

A study like this is necessary, to proclaim women's talents.

CHANGES IN LANGUAGE SINCE THE 1960S

Views and theories on language have progressed considerably in this short period. The step forward in the 1960s publicising women's issues has not been followed by the usual step back which undermined so many women's movements hitherto. On the contrary, it was consolidated by consciousness-raising groups and legislation. Patriarchal linguistic usage limiting women is being continually questioned. The 1960s achievements of Lessing, Drabble and McCarthy in printing their feelings even about menstruation and contraception were built on by radical feminists, notably Dale Spender in *Man Made Language*.[2] Her forthright theory is that men control the meaning of words and are thus able to impose their view of the world on everyone; women, without the ability to symbolise their experience in the dominant male discourse, either internalise male reality and feel marginalised in our society, or are unable to express their feelings. The word 'silence' appears in many book titles.[3]

Feminist literary critics point out that women developed strategies for dealing with marginalisation either by sharing with other women, or through writing, or by developing their own subcultures (no longer devalued by patriarchal terms such as 'gossip'). Discourse which had been pilloried – such as the talk of black mothers in the kitchen – is studied by their daughters for its rich imagery, rhythms and political comment. Strategies are continually devised to make our language reconceptualise us. Weldon used punch-lines such as 'Down among the Women' almost as Blake used 'Damn

braces' to make us rethink our attitudes. Like feminist
linguists, she wants to free women from the idle discourse
which merely accepts prevailing conventions and therefore
maintains them.[4]

Women are adapting male theories to free themselves.
Freud's views on female passivity are rejected in favour of
his insights into the way our unconscious makes images –
that feminists are exploring to speed liberation from their
thrall. Structuralist theory might have been allowed to mystify
by its vocabulary, and exclude women, as so many disciplines
have done in the past. But instead, it has been exploited to
demonstrate how meaning is constructed culturally, and can
thus be deconstructed, to reconstruct us.

This freeing of language has allowed many more languages
to flourish. We have overcome the privileging of white
patriarchal discourse to revalue 'dialects' for their diversity;
and to see women writing in many different forms of English,
from Bessie Head in South Africa, poeticising her own and
her people's suffering, to middle-class Indians, such as Anita
Desai, voicing world-wide feminist longings for liberation.[5]

We have progressed in two decades from perceiving
language as limiting us to conceiving language as constructing
us. (There is a fascinating passage showing this happening
when Frederica falls in love in *Still Life* (1985) by Antonia
Byatt.) Unthinking acceptance of others' definitions goes with
reluctance to question our social system. Reflection about
language is politically progressive in the sense that it makes
issues public and insists on changes in usage.

When Charlotte Brontë described a plain, poor girl, worthy
of a rich, masterful, inteligent man, she wrote into our
discourse (and our unconscious) a new potential for previously
marginalised women. When Drabble, Figes and Weldon
discuss female bodily functions openly, they are deconstructing some of the Judaeo-Christian mythology which hitherto
shamed women.

WOMEN NOVELISTS AND 'REALISM'

In the late 1980s we are at a stimulating stage where we accept widely differing views of the world (ideologies) and the novel, from realism to deconstruction, from humanism to anti-humanism. The writer makes an experiential world, within a convention and against it. But our concept of mimesis (imitation of reality) has been questioned so frequently that we cannot do anything the same again.

Realism is a mode with assumptions that many find harder to accept. History and mass extermination have depersonalised the individual. Thus Kurt Vonnegut and Fay Weldon play with depersonalised protagonists, yet for completely different reasons. He is pessimistically wry about humanity; she is optimistically wry about female futures. Today, all forms of the novel are equally privileged – fabulation as prominent as traditional forms. For women, so often misrepresented in male writing, representation is as important as fabulation. Women, from middle-class white to working-class and black, have revitalised the realistic novel by using it to explore and share their experience. Art orders the contingency of experience, and gives women a short-lived, badly needed control over their lives.

The women novelists who adapt traditional forms to interpret their lives have this in common with radical thinkers: they make language re-envisage the world. What some anti-humanists underestimate is the continuing need for the humanist novel and its discourse to represent the complexity and variousness of women. This is valid alongside those works which privilege, almost for the first time, the 'wild' zone of specifically female experience (such as the novels by Michèle Roberts). The modern writer makes art – realist and non-realist – out of the exploration of the relation between a unique life and the body of literature and the world. The novel is a language world; modern realism is webbed in with our dark, contemporary sense of broken connections between the individual and society, the conscious and the unconscious. The laws of realism are inherent in many texts that question them, while the 'imagination' has always been anxious about its link with the facts of the world.

FEMINIST LITERARY CRITICISM

This stimulating diversity has contributed to the new discipline of feminist literary criticism. Anglo-American literary critics exploit a wide range of theory, whenever they consider it useful, from psychoanalytic to Marxist, structuralist to humanist. Feminist criticism is centrally concerned with questioning the place of women's writing in the existing system of values, just as feminists question the situation of women in society generally. Are there ways of writing, thinking and reading which are specific to women?[6]

Women's experience is the firm, shared territory in spite of wide differences. 'Experience' is not just a personal sequence of thoughts but shares that of other women as they consider the text in a vital and productively new relation to it. The pathmaking feminist literary critics worked in American universities. They look with fresh eyes at the ways women wrote in the nineteenth century, and unearth frustrations, an implicit hatred of patriarchy, female metaphors and sexual symbolism, omissions, ideologies hitherto unsuspected. The most interesting are also the easiest to read: Elaine Showalter, *A Literature of Their Own* (Princeton University Press, 1977; Virago, 1978); Ellen Moers, *Literary Women* (Women's Press, 1978); Patricia Spacks, *The Female Imagination* (Allen and Unwin, 1976); and Sandra Gilbert and Susan Gubar, *The Madwoman in the Attic* (University of Yale Press, 1979).

Reading as a woman helps to overcome former reading when everyone was expected to read like a man, above all in college courses. Male response had concealed much, alienated many women from themselves by presenting male experience as the human one. The hypothesis of a woman reader displaces the dominant male vision and reveals the masks of truth (as in many of Murdoch's novels) with which patriarchy hides its fictions. Men critics can accept such readings since they are a critique of inequalities. They provide rational and serious rereadings of aspects previously omitted or distorted. (For example, showing how the eighteenth-century novel, however innovative, reconciled courtly romanticising of female

sexuality within a restrictive, Puritan idealisation of marriage.)
This reinterpretation is fundamental, often a revision.

LITERARY CRITICISM TODAY

Literary criticism has displaced philosophy as a source for
our self-description, our analysis of being. Literary theory
has this central role because literature takes as its subject all
human experience. Literature orders, interprets and articu-
lates the relations between men and women, the puzzling
manifestations of the human psyche, the effects of material
conditions on human experience. The comprehensiveness of
literature makes it possible for extraordinary and compelling
theory to be drawn into literary theory. It invites discussions
of rationality, intelligibility, even what the 'individual' means.

Literary criticism was given academic respectability and
useful vocabulary by the New Critics in America. They
concentrate not on the author but on the text, its 'subtlety'
and 'unity'. One of the shrewdest was Empson who, in his
Seven Types of Ambiguity, laid the way for the complex
distinctions of structuralism. Though much criticised by
Marxists for neglecting the social conditions under which
texts are produced, the New Criticism, expounded forcefully
by Leavis, Iris Murdoch and T.S. Eliot, and taught us in
school, did begin to theorise about interpretation. Structuralism goes further and gives scientific method to the study of
literary structures and discourses (codes). This wide term
transformed literary criticism thanks to the imaginative
demythologising of Barthes, Foucault and Todorov.[7]

In *Mythologies* (1957; English translation 1972), Barthes
expounds the ways in which ideology masquerades as truth,
and pervades the discourse, images and myths of twentieth-
century society. Languages and structures rather than an
'author' become the major source of explanation. Marxists
see it as a complete break with the past because it is anti-
humanist in no longer considering man the centre of his
world (decentring him).[8] However, structuralism can be
viewed as a continuation, not necessarily a rejection – because
it often deals with different 'texts' including those not

previously in the literary canon, such as advertising.

If we allow the modern reader's right to interpret, then no theory should be excluded. We live in an age which boasts as great a creativity in criticism as in fiction!

THE CRITICAL APPROACH OF THIS STUDY

My approach is determinedly eclectic. In the late 1980s we see that each theory has much to offer, while on its own it can prove limiting – if not for its greatest exponents, for many of its followers. It is a tribute to the women writers here that a diversity of critical approaches is not only helpful but needed. Each critical theory has concepts and vocabulary which are useful, often illuminating, but restrictive without the insights of other theories. This is partly because we can never fully grasp our own ideological attitude and therefore need openness to what we might be inclined to ignore. Humanist literary criticism privileges the historical expressiveness of realism, analysed through 'plot' and 'character'. Structuralism provides a more systematic review of structures and an exalting of the reader's role in interpretation. Marxist critics insist we question, like feminists, the conditions of production which influence not only the writer but the book in a capitalist society. Deconstruction has taught us that many of our ideas are socially[9] *constructed*, especially through writing, and can therefore be deconstructed in our literary criticism.

These movements since structuralism may be termed postmodernist in rejecting the notion of man as the primary origin of meaning and value.[10] Such anti-humanism has made some thinkers nihilistic about the future. However, if we adopt the moral approach of novelists and feminists we can read the postmodern debunking of humanism as a protest against the inhumanity of our times. Feminism offers a revaluation of half the human race through the 'images of women' approach, the reappraisal of women's novels, and theories of gender difference in reading, writing and literary interpretation. The respect for the 'other' required in everyday life and the novel asserts the positive aspects of humanist *and* antihumanist criticism.[11] The goal of criticism today is to read the text as an explanation of writing *and* of the problems of articulating our world. What greater objective can a critic have?

THE SIX WRITERS IN THIS STUDY

The six writers in this book have been chosen because their work represents six different attitudes to the novel, to the world, and above all to the varied links between sexuality and language since the 1960s. Their different attitudes mirror the novel's development: Iris Murdoch wishes to revive the richness of nineteenth-century prose, as used by Dickens and Dostoyevsky. She includes women's concerns, from spiritual longings to gossip about motivation; but her ideological position is that language can and should be divorced from gender identification. Antonia Byatt interweaves the discourses of science and structuralism with discourses of feeling. She is interested in the analysis of male as well as female sexuality; like Coleridge and Virginia Woolf, she believes that the artist's mind should be androgynous, capable of masculine and feminine. Murdoch and Byatt share the view of the radical feminist Kristéva (though from differing standpoints) that feminine and masculine attributes are fluid, not possessed by one sex alone, but present in all avantgarde artists.

Margaret Drabble represents the frustrations of many women writers of the 1960s (often mothers) who created realist fictions about themselves. Their language does not attempt androgyny, since it centres on female preoccupations, from the double bind to a mother's sense of guilt; it proudly includes mention of the female body and its influence. Fay Weldon goes further, including the humiliations experienced by the female body and using these to politicise areas such as sexuality, marriage and childrearing. She realises the pull of biological, economic and linguistic conditioning in her own life, and represents the tensions felt by women as they try to conform or free themselves from conflicting images. Her language is the most incisively feminist, since she exploits the punch-lines of advertising to make us rethink women's lives. Murdoch provided theoretical support for their use of language in 'Against Dryness' (1961). She claims that a novelist representing 'real' individuals struggling in society can think in degrees of freedom – an aim of both recent linguistic theory and feminism.[12]

Figes represents the experimental voice. She is in the tradition of some of the greatest twentieth-century novel-writing which is non-realist, from Joyce to Beckett. She explores alternative meanings for women through polemic and through modernist metaphor. Kristéva considers the modernism of writers like Woolf and Joyce revolutionary in its fragmentation. Figes combines 'feminine' or semiotic elements from Woolf and Sarraute to talk of women's bodily experiences. She focuses a questioning spotlight on the previous exclusion of women, a spotlight which heightened language awareness. The exhilaration felt by many women writers led to the creating of new subject-matter in new forms, exemplified by *Waking*. Michelene Wandor expresses her feelings and those of other writers in 1968:

> There was a new seriousness. Gender self-consciousness was central to what impelled me to write. There is so much potential for women writers at the moment that I see an expansion in horizons and options. Feminist poetry has brought out a new audience; plays are being written by women that could not have been written ten years ago. Feminist writing can be useful to ordinary women, as it shows the female soul and its qualities.[13]

PATRIARCHAL ATTITUDES BY EVA FIGES

Patriarchal Attitudes by Eva Figes, published in 1970, helped change the attitudes of many English women. She had intended to write a book about women but found that almost all the words, all the books about women had been written by men. As Virginia Woolf commented: 'So consistently has the author been male . . . that the moment a women sets pen to paper . . . she is accused of bias'(*A Room of One's Own*, p.6). Women's language and meaning has been decreed by men, with the male as norm. The male-as-norm has permeated all systems of knowledge, which must now be deconstructed if we are to liberate ourselves.

Figes analyses weaknesses in male reasoning and offers a definition of thought which avoids the dichotomy between rationality and irrationality, male and female. 'We guess, we assume, we construct false theories, moving forward in the only way possible, fumbling in the dark' (p.19). A definition, interestingly, taken from the structuralist Lévi-Strauss, in *Totemism and the Savage Mind*.

Figes researched widely to support the argument that nurture is more important than nature in the construction of femininity. 'The image in the mirror to which we dance is created by Man; not by men and women jointly for common ends . . . Man's vision of women is not objective, but an uneasy combination of what he wishes her to be and what he fears her to be' (p.16). This is a novelistic image to support her polemic. Figes turned from argument to the novel to analyse what woman feels like, to see how far identity is connected with biology. In *Days*, and above all in *Waking*, Figes represents different stages in a woman's life through her bodily feelings. She achieves a breakthrough in language to represent women's mental and physical sensations. She is liberating language from the shame shrouding the female body. Like the French feminist Luce Irigaray, Figes maintains that previously women had no way of representing themselves and suggests they start with their body, their sexuality. For women to discover who they are they must begin with their femaleness as a source of self-knowledge.

ANITA BROOKNER

Brookner represents the old dichotomy between male and female, with men getting the best out of life. She sees gender psychology, accentuated by the eighteenth-century novel, as still continuing to limit women. So her heroines, however intelligent, are restricted by their sentiment, their gentleness, their sense of duty, whereas her male characters are freer emotionallly and can live by their own logic. Her women feel they must repress desire, they define themselves as lack, as non-being. They are marginalised not only by society but by their unconscious image of themselves as merely subjects-on-trial. Her discourse would be categorised as 'feminine' by Kristéva: 'using what is traditionally considered feminine (sensations, colours etc.) and a certain sensitivity to language, to its phonetic texture, its logical articulation . . . and ideological conflicts of our time' (*Feminine Writing*, p.167).

Brookner may be termed 'post-feminist' as she understands the old restrictions, but sees them still reigning in the psyche as well as society. Her protagonists have a limited range of options, they are not at home in the late twentieth century. Brookner stated in interview: 'A lot of people are bewildered by the feminist propaganda fed them.' She shows, in the unfulfilled bodies of her heroines, that oppressiveness has not withered. A study of her is illuminating in that she treats the 'woman's' novel seriously, *and* is extremely popular, with *Hotel du Lac* topping sales for a year, not needing the help of women's presses.

Hers is the category of fiction, written mainly by women, with women readers in mind. Nicola Beauman, in *A Very Great Profession* (1983), defines its 'female tone of voice, little action and less histrionics, the drama of the undramatic' (p.5). It deals with daily life *and* intense emotions; its ideology is that the novel mirrors life. It tells the reader what women thought and felt, it illuminates female attitudes and underprivileged experience. It too frequently advocates self-abnegation, yet at times with implicit anger. Its strength is to foreground the importance of human relationships – vital if we are to survive.

CONCLUSION

The novelists in this study have been chosen for their diversity of voice, not their homogeneity. Nevertheless there are features they all share: they all experiment responsibly and excitingly with literary language, they are committed to re-thinking its use. They struggle to diversify English language in the novel – as it is being wrestled with in Africa and India, to make new statements about the world. They have mostly been to university and can use dominant (male) discourse.

They can also move in and out of feminist approaches. Four of them are mothers and include maternal (and bodily) preoccupations.

They take love as central, indeed Murdoch views it as essential to characterisation. Marriage is problematic, but the capacity to relate to others is a value by which their 'characters' are judged – and most of the men found wanting.

They are respected by critics and have achieved public recognition. Most of them can (just) live on their earnings. These statements reveal much about the type of novels women want to read – and fiction readers are mainly women. Furthermore, women novelists demonstrate a diversity which challenges traditional categorisations. They show that the gap between humanistic realism and the experimental novel is not as great as anti-humanists (marxists, structuralists and deconstructionists) would have us believe. Nor is the concept of 'character' dead if we are truthful in our analysis of the way we treat each other in everyday conversation – or novel-reading. The six novelists here demonstrate the richness of voices, topics and structures in women's writing today.

NOTES

Unless otherwise stated, the books cited are published in London.
1. Patriarchy is a much-debated term. Marxist-feminists wish to retain it for its social critique, whereas many others find it problematical. For further discussion see *M/F*, 82/83. Veronica Beechey, *Feminist Review* (no. 3) gives the various conflicting meanings the word assumes in feminist discourses.
2. Dale Spender, *Man Made Language* (Routledge, 1980), is clear and polemical. She uses patriarchy to denote the social structures where men control power and define areas of knowledge.
3. Such as Adrienne Rich, *Lies, Secrets and Silence* (Virago, 1980); Tillie Olsen, *Silences* (Virago, 1980); she comments: 'One out of 12: Writers who are women'.
4. See Deborah Cameron, *Feminism and Linguistic Theory* (Macmillan, 1985). She successfully charts sometimes obscure theory and shows how it can help to radicalise the language of the underprivileged.
5. I feel guilty about not mentioning many outstanding women writers in Africa, India and South America. They demand another book.
6. For a useful account of feminist perspectives, see Hester Eisenstein,

Contemporary Feminist Thought (Unwin Paperback, 1985); Elaine Showalter, *The New Feminist Criticism* (Virago, 1986) provides a range of recent essays displaying a stimulating diversity of opinions. Maggie Humm, *Feminist Criticism: Women as Contemporary Critics* (Harvester Press, 1986) explores the main features of feminist critical theory.

7. One could describe these movements as swinging from humanism to anti-humanism, from modernism to postmodernism, from structuralism to post-structuralism (as in late Barthes). Indeed, one could posit a dialectical movement, for which I propose a synthesis in the ethical imagination (of novelists and feminists above all). Or one could claim to see, like Derrida, an unnecessarily exclusive metaphysical binary opposition. See Kate Soper, *Humanism and Anti-Humanism* (Hutchinson, 1985).

8. The marxist critic Lukács used humanist vocabulary. The younger marxist critics, such as Terry Eagleton, term themselves anti-humanist. He gives a forceful account of his approach in *Marxism and Literary Theory* (Methuen, 1977).

9. Or rather textually inscribed in discourses; these discursive forms can be antithetical to the 'social'.

10. There is a useful article by F. Jameson, 'Postmodernism or the Cultural Logic of Late Capitalism', *New Left Review*, no. 145 (1978).

11. For a philosophical elaboratioon of this I recommend Dr Richard Kearney, *The Wake of Imagination: Ideas of Creativity in Western Culture* (Hutchinson, 1987).

12. Toril Moi, *Feminist Literary Theory* (Methuen, 1985) is a bold, short analysis of the strengths and weaknesses of contemporary feminists, ending with a demand for theory as necessary to clarify future thinking.

13. Michelene Wandor, *Gender and Writing* (Pandora, 1983).

CHAPTER 1
Iris Murdoch
Moralist for Our Time

Iris Murdoch has never wanted to be called a 'woman writer', preferring to be accepted as a writer in a man's world. This reflects the desire of women of her generation (she was born in 1919) to be accepted as equal, not different. It was not till the 1960s, and even more the 1970s, that many women expressed the need to stress gender difference. Iris Murdoch has never felt this need; like Virginia Woolf and Simone de Beauvoir, she considers good art should transcend gender difference. She claims that: 'The novel is about facing up to the truth and living with a more realistic view of oneself and other people.'[1] This moral concern, together with her joyful inventiveness, make Murdoch a major British novelist. Her twenty-four novels present remarkably imagined characters through whom she examines the complexities of relationships – and art.

I intend to look at Iris Murdoch as a novelist, a moralist and from a feminist point of view. Feminist perspectives illuminate some of her unusual qualities: her ability to inhabit a male psyche; her use of a dominant male voice together with more questioning voices; her respect for partial failures, for the flawed individual.

She is committed to the realistic depiction of individuals; a characteristically English realism which depends on love, in author and reader, towards the characters. In 'Against Dryness' (1961)[2] she advocates the 'liberal' English tradition of respect for the individual. A.S. Byatt (who has written one of the most incisive studies of Murdoch's novels in *Degrees of Freedom*, 1965) considers 'Against Dryness' the most compelling defence of liberalism, of 'real, various individuals struggling in society'. Murdoch assumes that one of the novel's tasks is to create realistically perceived characters and to transmit moral judgements through their relationships. Thus she can be considered in the tradition of female creators of the novel in the eighteenth century, such as Fanny Burney and Jane Austen.

Her respect for character is based on a moral and philosophical view: that we should give full attention to other individuals, in life as in the novel. 'Attention' is a term taken from Simone Weil, the French philosopher whom she admires. It suggests the need to forget one's personality in order to look seriously at other people. 'Good art can't help teaching you things, but it shouldn't aim at teaching,' asserts Murdoch.[3] It should not aim at teaching, as the novel is a literary artefact, a work of the imagination. She possesses a modern realisation of the paradoxes of realism: that it attempts to represent the world 'as it is', which is virtually impossible, given the limits of our minds and our language.

She self-consciously combines realistic descriptions of people with half-fantastic plots. She is a fabulator in that she takes especial pleasure in design and invention; a theorist in proclaiming that the novel should return to the often questioned idea of character. She pioneers the unfashionable concept of art as knowledge, based on humanistic realism. Murdoch's realism is not unlike Aristotle's mimesis, which states that art is an imitation of reality. One of her objectives is the vivid rendering of the world of individual centres of consciousness we live in. This leads her to maintain, like Plato, that 'bad art is a lie about the world'. In this she is in the mainstream of English literary criticism since Leavis – a mainstream dismissed by Marxists and structuralists for implicitly supporting capitalism. They object to realism as assuming a non-contradictory individual. But attention to Murdoch's statements reveals a complex view of the individual as frequently contradictory, seldom unified. For this reason I quote many of her declarations, not to support the intentional school of criticism which pays too much attention to authors' intentions, but because a shrewd commentator like Murdoch can increase the subtlety of our exploration of her works.

Admittedly, realist narrative moves towards some sense of order in its endings when decisive choices are often made. Structuralists see this as underwriting capitalist ideology in stressing consumer choice. But a close reading of some of Murdoch's comments such as, 'It is difficult to overestimate the amount of illusion in any human soul',[4] reveals a fairly pessimistic view of human freedom. Furthermore, her endings suggest how limited our choices are, how circumscribed our potential. The traditional novel is far more critical of the status quo than many modern critics allow.

She is aware of the difficulties involved in realism, yet expresses explicit moral attachment to its values. She loves to create habitable imagined worlds while commenting on their fictiveness. Some of her best novels can be read as fables about the difficulties of realism and truth-telling. Her first published novel (*Under the Net*, 1954) demonstrates the ambiguous power of the tradition, the curiously symbiotic relationship between old realism and new experiment. It is a conceptual game about the need for concepts, yet a serious disquisition on the limits of realism. 'Literature represents a battle between real people and images.'[5]

THE TENSION BETWEEN REALISM AND FABULATION

Murdoch's fiction might be defined as a battle between real people and fantasy. She delights in games-playing and fabulation, which she usually succeeds in grounding with realistically drawn characters. She uses the philosophically respectable term 'games-playing', rather than 'fantasy' which can reveal subversive elements. Our culture has attempted to silence unreason and otherness by interpreting fantasy as moral allegory – a valid approach to Murdoch's plots. Nevertheless, she is subversive in allowing us to cross frontiers into the unconscious and enjoy forbidden, dark areas; like the civil servants performing black magic in basements, in *The Nice and the Good* (1968).

Though many refer to her plotting as contrived, her contrivances usually arise from the psychological problems of her characters and can thus be justified from a realistic standpoint: Priscilla in *The Black Prince* (1973) (subsequently referred to as *BP*) finally commits suicide, just as her brother, unsuccessful in planning his life, has begun to make love to Julian. The characters undergo real ordeals, symbolising the cruelty of chance, or fake ordeals, as tests. Adventures test character, but seem mainly introduced because Murdoch enjoys fabulation, invention; in *Nuns and Soldiers* (1980) there are two near-drownings, similar to one undergone by Murdoch herself, intensely dramatic, even sensational.

It must be remembered that sensationalism was an element in the nineteenth-century novels Murdoch admires, from Dickens to Dostoyevsky. It can be used to express disillusion with the idea of historical progress. Furthermore, the 'uncanny' may bring to the surface unconscious desires and hates which threaten society's taboos. The sea-monster in *The Sea, The Sea* (1978) symbolises the protagonist's monstrous destructive jealousy as it erupts into his self-congratulatory journal. From a Marxist perspective, such fantastic sequences question bourgeois realism. Such disrupting of the realistic mode either weakens the structure, as in *The Nice and the Good*, or enriches it, as in her latest novel *The Good Apprentice*.

Here the threatening house and eerie woods recall the sensational, uncanny sequences in gothic novels. The gothic has its roots in the literature of unreason, it establishes a rhetoric of fantasy to speak the socially unspeakable. The three beautiful women caught in the isolated gothic house of *The Good Apprentice* feel passion and hatred for the famous painter father they are forced to nurse. The desires they cannot realise within our culture are expressed by their potions and rituals. Murdoch's characters who indulge in black magic, like Nan's daughter in *The Sandcastle* (1957), represent forbidden longings. The gothic presentation of the family in *The Good Apprentice* conveys the oppressiveness of this social institution – a Marxist would point to the crippling effects of capitalism on our emotional and psychic life; but Murdoch would echo Plato in representing fantasy as a weakness in our psyche.

Nevertheless she enjoys the constructing of fantastic plots, demonstrating the mobility of our fantasy. Her artifice and complex plotting could be said to ally her with Anne Radcliffe's female gothic. She justifies her apparently contradictory aims by maintaining that we 'all synthesise fact, fiction and allegory'.[6] Yet she does not always achieve this synthesis in her writing. Her practice sometimes runs counter to her theories; she maintains that life has no meaning or pattern, yet her plots impose patterns exploring uncontrollable forces in our subconscious. She admits her contradictions: 'Art represents the temptation to impose form . . . morality has to do with *not* imposing form'.[7]

In the main she manages the almost contradictory novelistic feat of marrying realism and fabulation, the plausible and the implausible. And implausible coincidences certainly occur; these can be defended realistically, since coincidences occur in life – or aesthetically – as a tidy plot can prove unexciting. Violence erupts in her novels, as it does on our television screens; and is studied from psychic and psychological viewpoints in *The Philosopher's Pupil* (1982). A disturbed pubescent girl dances in the uncanny wood of *The Good Apprentice*; the uncanny represents the psyche not at home in the world. It reflects Murdoch's concern with flawed individuals, those who suffer from 'cosmic homelessness', like Anne in *Nuns and Soldiers*. Anne has a vision of Christ, an undramatic Christ with a down-to-earth moral message; the supernatural is made credible, the subconscious is made homely. Murdoch's narrative works towards the imposition of form, with imagery suggested by the unconscious forces in our psyche. At the same time her structures work towards the painful awareness of moral imperatives, a partial acquisition of self-knowledge. She bravely, almost alone defends art as the instrument of knowledge, of morality.

MURDOCH'S MORAL PHILOSOPHY

The prominence she gives to morality is rare in the twentieth century, while her interest in 'virtue' is unusual in moral philosophy today. She analyses our longing for the Good through flawed characters. Most male philosophers (except perhaps Hume) have preferred abstract moral theory which she eschews in favour of seeing how precepts work in practice. It was claimed in the past that it is feminine to prefer experience to system-building. Her strength – like Jane Austen's – argued the Oxford philosopher Ryle in *Oxford Review*,[8] is to analyse the dilemmas caused by conflicting moral principles in ordinary situations.

Murdoch maintains there is a difference between her writing of philosophy (which should use the apparently impersonal language of argument and reason) and her fiction-writing. Certainly, she achieves admirable clarity in her expositions of the ideas of Sartre, and Plato in *The Sovereignty of Good* (1970); and *The Fire and the Sun* (1977) is a lucid exposition of Plato's views on art. Yet one is uncertain to what extent she is refuting or sympathising with it since she is fascinated by the paradoxical coexistence of puritan and artist in Plato – a paradox often echoed in her own writing.

Her first book on philosophy was published in 1953: *Sartre: romantic rationalist*. It offers a brilliant placing of Sartre's thought. However his novels – understandably – interest her as much as his philosophy: 'The novelist has implicitly understood what the philosopher has grasped less clearly that human reason is not a single unitary gadget the nature of which could be discovered once for all . . . in consequence has often anticipated the philosophers' discoveries' (p.8), asserts Murdoch.

The language of philosophy has been called 'the discourse of discourses'. It holds mastery, pre-eminence, like scientific discourse. The systems of representation at work are speculative, self-reflexive in ignoring woman; sometimes called 'masculine' by feminists. Given Murdoch's insistence of the difference between writing fiction and writing philosophy, and her distinctive discourse in each, it is valuable to look at these distinctions.

THE MALE NARRATOR

Murdoch is intriguing as a novelist in preferring to use male narrators. The claim to write like a man involves the playing of a role. Feminists such as Luce Irigaray see role-playing as central to the female subverting of male discourse. 'Mimetism, an acting out of role-playing within the text allows the woman writer the bettter to know and hence expose what she mimics.'[9]

Murdoch exposes the lack of self-knowledge, the weaknesses of her male narrators through their own words. She eschews the anger which feminist critics such as Gilbert and Gubar[10] have noted as implicit in many female texts. This may be because her use of different discourses allows her to cross gender boundaries, thus gaining access to the male psyche as well as the female. She sees what moral preoccupations they share as much as the psychological fantasies that separate. She encapsulates cerebration and emotion, mind and body, philosophy and poetry. She examines these traditional divisions in western culture through her male narrators *and* her own authorial voice.

Her male characters often fail to 'see' as they talk too much, like Charles in *The Sea, the Sea*. Such word-children are unreliable narrators, artistically gifted, but frustrated by their misuse of their gifts. Fantasising is linked with the gift of articulacy – a danger in her own novels, which results in the occasional purple passage. She makes the males realise how much they have to learn, how much they play roles. They gain a plurality of vision as they learn. Charles' self-congratulatory journal provides a commentary on his egotism, which circumstances force him to face. She subverts male models of behaviour by showing the protagonist having to revise his assumptions about women, about personal power, about maleness and femaleness. The questing male hero is treated ironically. But when he is humiliated it is not so much because he is male, but for living too much in illusion. Murdoch believes facing up to reality equally important, and difficult, for *all* of us. For her the pursuit of the Good transcends gender boundaries.

She proves that it does *not* inhibit female creativity to write like a man (as some feminists have claimed).[11] Indeed, the mask of male narrator allows her to explore areas seldom dealt with by women: the sexual and erotic experience of men, examined generously through the ageing Bradley in *The Black Prince*, and the homosexual Michael in *The Bell* (1958), among many others. Like Freud, she considers libidinal energy to be at the base of artistic, erotic and spiritual experience.

USE OF LANGUAGE

However her imagery for this experience is different for her male and female characters. She shows the gulf between men and women as they fall in love. Her female characters often use poignantly inadequate clichés of magazine romance to express their longings, like Midge: 'Oh for freedom, to be out of this cage of lies and pain at last! She looked into her dressing-table mirror, at her beautiful hair and distorted face, and for a moment opened her eyes wide and resumed her old insistent animated look which said, "like me, like me",'[12] For such women, limited by cultural images of themselves, the experience of love often involves defeat. They may be caught in a relationship to a selfish man, like the women in *The Black Prince* or (in gothic mode) shut up by father or lover like Hannah in *The Unicorn*, or the young ward in *The Philosopher's Pupil* (1982).

There is a large cast of unappreciated females, frequently living in houses where they have few rights. The image of the house has been used in female writing since eighteenth-century gothic and Jane Austen to suggest both enclosure and possible salvation.

Nevertheless the 'wild' zone of specifically female experience is not one that concerns Murdoch. Like Simone de Beauvoir she uses male metaphors to show distaste for the female body and its secretions. She eschews mention of the especially feminine, long-term caring love of mothers. It might be claimed that she is 'female' in stressing the self-abnegation of a writer. However she would deny feminists' stress on gender-identification since she maintains that all artists should

aim at impersonality; and that all human beings should learn
to think less of self.

In *The Black Prince* she can be identified both with the
prolific Baffin and with Bradley, who personifies her ideal of
impersonality in writing, together with her belief in a long
apprenticeship. (She did not publish her first novel until she
was 37, though she had written many before that, which she
hid away.) The tragi-grotesque Bradley writes Murdochian
prose which he despises: 'thin layered stuff of ironic sensibility
. . . if I were a fictive character, would be that much deeper
and denser.' But she is also the editor Loxias (Apollo) who
points to the limits of our language. She stresses the limits
of our language, almost like post-structuralists, but the
fertility of her imagination leads to different conclusions. The
very inadequacy of language helps her to create novels out
of unending approximations of words: 'The human task has
become a literary task'.[13] Since structuralism one might
rephrase this as 'the human task has become a linguistic
task'.

THE NOVEL AS COMIC FORM

'Language is a comic form. God, if he existed, would laugh
at his creation. Yet it is also the case that life is horrible,
without metaphysical sense, wrecked by chance, pain and
the close prospect of death. Out of this is born irony, our
dangerous and necessary tool' (*BP*, p.81). Since Jane Austen,
it has been acknowledged that irony is well deployed by
women. It can prove a subtle weapon, since the intended
meaning is the opposite of the one stated. Murdoch's first-
person male narrators always begin with partial delusions,
exposed relentlessly. There is ghoulish irony at the end of
The Black Prince when each character claims to have been
loved by Bradley and to know the truth. Or the irony can
be gentle, as when Bradley says of his unproductiveness: 'Art
has its martyrs, not least those who have preserved their
silence' (p.11). Irony is especially useful to underline the
discrepancy between our intentions and our actions, our
conscious and our subconscious.

In spite of her serious intentions, Murdoch considers the novel essentially a comic form; comic because even at our most solemn moments we may appear absurd to an onlooker. She represents her characters as 'mortal, limited, absurd, contingent – and this belongs to a comic world'.[14] Though still writing on philosophy, she insists that there are few philosophical concepts in her novels. One only needs to grasp that 'contingent' means not necessary to any purpose on the world. 'It's because we are only contingent, or I prefer to say accidental, that we have so little dignity. That is why I consider the novel essentially comic in vision. Tragedy is an art form rarely used, demanding poetry.'[15] The term comedy is ample, including both humour and 'the human comedy' in the sense of Dante and Shakespeare.

Her best novels are often the funniest. Since the first she has shown her mastery at farce, slapstick, parody and black humour. Slapstick is an area where women have not been allowed to perform till recently; it both underlines the silliness of our illusions *and* her insistence that art is about illusion and reality. *Under the Net* includes hilarious scenes, such as the attempts to capture an ageing, caged filmstar dog and the crumpling of a cardboard filmset. Such slapstick – the physical intrusion of the absurd – imparts a sense of happiness. More importantly, the psychological machinery of humour is often egalitarian. We are *all* capable of behaving like automata, as Bergson pointed out in *Le rire* – especially when in love.

LOVE

Falling in love is central to Murdoch's plots, as it is to many women's novels. She uses falling in love to examine character and morality. She has taken the age-old female limitation – life circumscribed to caring for and loving those nearest – and turned it into a moral guide. 'And what should concern us more than love? in the sense of what connects one with the natural world. That is energy. There's nothing strange in making that central.'[16]

She is eloquent on erotic love, reintroducing some of the richness of nineteenth-century prose when she includes elements of romantic worship and idealisation. But she tests her characters by the ways they respond, and finds most of them wanting, incapable of giving themselves honestly, or seeing the other clearly for long.

Murdoch exploits falling in love to discover appalling truths. Like Jane Austen, she considers the way one loves reveals personality. Loving involves lies, hypocrisy, even secrecy, so provides a useful tool for wider social analysis, the 'stuff' of life essential to this type of novel. Through it she can also analyse the secretive parts of our mind, not entirely subconscious, not entirely fantasy. She offers shrewd studies of obsessiveness, such as our urge to lie (as in Tim in *Nuns and Soldiers*, who hates his lying, only redeemed by his ability to love).

Love is the touchstone by which her characters are judged, as in Shakespeare's comedies. She praises Shakespeare for his 'extraordinary ability to combine a marvellous pattern or myth with the expansion of characters as absolutely free persons, independent of each other'.[17] Both these writers use our foolishness and devotion when in love to construct comic works of art.

Falling in love is a convenient *dramatic* device containing suspense, surprise, theatrical coincidence, even violence. 'Dramas happen when there is trouble . . . . To dramatise your life represents a very general human temptation.'[18] And she derives form, like many women novelists, from the process of falling in love: it provides a variety of patterns in the slow or speedy meeting of two people, their spiritual or erotic or failed union, followed by life together or misery at forced or involuntary partings. These patterns are too often criticised. They demonstrate the need she shares with experimentalists to play with the shaping of fictions. 'Art is playing games,' she and her characters frequently state. Like John Barth and other American experimentalists, she enjoys the ludic quality in art, well symbolised by the absurdity of characters in erotic positions. Barth in *Chimera* (1982) incorporates Scheherezade's storytelling (and sexual exploitation) from *Arabian Nights* to muse about the imagination's need to borrow and adapt stores. Inventive plagiarism is also set against the violence of sudden death in *The Black Prince* with its echoes of *Hamlet* and allegorical patterns of love and destruction.

Murdoch is the only contemporary woman novelist to find inspiration in Plato's *The Symposium*. There he distinguishes between love or high Eros, and sex or low Eros. Both forms are energising, not mutually excluding. Indeed, Michael in *The Bell* (1958), admits that his religion and his homosexual passion 'both come from the same source' (p.99). Twenty-five years later the priest in *The Philosopher's Pupil* (1982) dedicates 'his love, that is, his sexuality' to God (p.156). This priest no longer feels the shame which destroyed Michael's happiness: 'Good is a sublimation of sexuality, not necessarily sexless.' Furthermore, 'All art is connected with sex.' She maintains that the structure of good literary works has to do with erotic mysteries. She makes poetic use of Plato, showing how sexual love of the beautiful can lead to the Good, to aesthetic and moral worth.

Freud has also affected her in that she considers libido central to the understanding of our unconscious motivation.

> There's a deep truth in certain things, like the notion of the *superego* and the *id*. What I agree with in Freud is the doctrine of the unconscious mind, and the idea of *eros* as fundamental energy, a drive which includes sex and which can be good and can be bad (that's all in Plato) . . . . Dreams have a great many sorts of explanation. Once the Freud virus has got into you, you keep looking at things in his way.[19]

Libido, erotic desire, is used symbolically to illustrate the universality of the id and represent aspects of sexual behaviour which are susceptible to generalisation and mythmaking. Unfortunately, the rich naturalistic texture of much of her writing makes it hard for many readers to accept the similarity of patterning in these loves. The characters are so distinct one expects their reactions to passion to be more varied, less symmetrical.

The Black Prince explores libidinal energy as the basis of artistic, erotic and spiritual experiences. Through her male narrator she represents the uncomfortable links between art, desire and sadomasochism; on two planes, through meditations on literary creativity, and through parody of popular Freudianism in the explanations of Marloe. Freud's comments on 'the true artist' give insights into her writing at its best: 'he understands how to work over his day-dreams in such a way as to make them lose what is too personal . . . he makes it possible for others to derive consolation and alleviation from their own sources of pleasure in their unconscious which have become inaccessible to them.'[20]

Murdoch finds Freud as useful to her writing as Plato since they both 'see Love as Energy. Libido can be good or bad but it is essentially sexual. Of course it can be dangerous or creative to fall in love.'[21] Eros can make for wholeness, as at the end of *The Black Prince*, but frequently proves demonic. She agrees with Freud's pessimistic view, 'Seeing the psyche as an egocentric system of quasi-mechanical energy, difficult to control'.[22] In *Nuns and Soldiers* libido increases the sense of loneliness and failure of the solitary Anne and the ingenuous, alienated Count. But it leads Anne at least to dedicate her life to others, to sublimate her passion.

Murdoch often represents feelings of love in religious terms, since these provide metaphors which can still be grasped by non-believers. The rapture of lovemaking gives rise to emotions not dissimilar to religious awe. She and her male narrators consider 'Man's creative struggle is a love story. The desire of the human heart for love and knowledge is infinite' (*BP*, p.366). This cosmic perspective links her with Marguerite Yourcenar, the greatest modern French woman writer.

MARGUERITE YOURCENAR

Yourcenar, in *Memoirs of Hadrian* (1951), sees Hadrian's love of physical beauty as an aspect of his wideranging mind. He is vaster in scope than any of Murdoch's characters, but shares their longing for knowledge, their desire to pursue good through fallible human love. Yourcenar's most gripping novel is *The Abyss* (not translated until 1984; the French title is *L'Oeuvre au noir*, 1968). It recreates a whole world – Europe in the sixteenth century – in order to examine the limits of human knowledge. Her protagonist, Zeno, has an overpowering desire to discover more about the physical world – at a time when scientific experiment was usually difficult, often forbidden. He experiments on the circulation of the blood, cures for the plague, power looms, even his own body; he is forced to flee from one country to another, to escape arrest. The threat he presents to rulers is that of dissident: he questions the systems and above all the theology of the time. This novel is both historical and relevant today, in that Zeno is persecuted by totalitarian regimes for being a thinker, an investigator, a writer.

He questions not only the existence of God, but the very bases of knowledge. Zeno was the Greek philosopher who pointed out the gulf between man's necessarily limited knowledge and his longing for the infinite. Furthermore, Zeno is an outsider in love as a homosexual in a narrow-minded society. He echoes the cosmic homelessness of the characters whom Murdoch most admires. Only through suffering do they find peace, after experiencing high and low Eros. Like the priest at the end of *The Philosopher's Pupil*, they learn an almost mystical detachment.

Hadrian's last musings have the perspective shown by Bradley:

> Life is atrocious we know. But precisely because I expect little of the human condition, man's periods of felicity, his partial progress, his efforts to begin over again and to continue, all seem to me like so many prodigies which nearly compensate for the monstrous mass of ills and defeats, of indifference and error. Catastrophe and ruin will come; disorder will triumph, but order will too, from time to time . . . not all our books will perish. (p.235)

Both Murdoch and Yourcenar share an admiration for Greek thought and the brief golden age when philosophy, rationality and the arts flourished. Yourcenar, the first woman elected to the French Academy, is immensely erudite, and includes much of her learning in her novels, which possibly accounts for her being undervalued in the English-speaking world. She and Murdoch share ideals influenced by Greek writers: to be just; to learn to die; to create something good. Though they might have been academic philosophers, both have preferred to create novels which analyse the moral problems of individuals.

Both foreground the study of the individual soul, like the nineteenth-century novel, but neither folllows it in presenting marriage as a solution or even possible salvation. They tend to depict heterosexual marriage as destructive. There are few happy sexual relationships in Murdoch or Yourcenar, and those few are nearly always homosexual, such as Zeno and his servant in *The Abyss*, and Axel and Simon in *A Fairly Honourable Defeat*. There is a link with certain feminists in Murdoch's portrayal of lesbian caring: Hernshaw and Seelhaft in *A Severed Head* (1961), and Mitzi and Charlotte in *An Accidental Man* (1971).

There has been little comment on Murdoch's understanding of the value of human bisexuality, yet it is striking how often she includes this feature, further emphasised by androgynous names. This appreciation of bisexuality provides a constructive link with the French feminist Julia Kristéva, though for different reasons: 'All speaking subjects have within them a certain bisexuality which is the possibility to explore all the sources of signification, that which posits a meaning as well as that which multiplies, pulverises and finally revives it.'[23] Furthermore, like many feminists of the 1970s, they divorce sexuality from maternity. Both childless, they are concerned with the adult's possibility of attaining spiritual grace through physical love – echoes both of Plato and Christianity.

RELIGION AND MAGIC

Tolstoy considered that a novel reflects the religious experience of an age. Certainly, Murdoch and Yourcenar depict people misusing or neglecting institutionalised religion, but longing for a more spiritual life.

Both analyse evil as intelligently as they analyse spirituality. Both point out how evil is produced by obsessive faiths (or fantasies), lack of self-knowledge, misplaced good intentions. In *The Abyss* there is a powerful evocation of the Anabaptists, their initial dignity, their final degradation in orgy. In both, evil takes on deceptive guises of greed, sloth, love of power, self-centredness in our morally messy world.

In Murdoch, evil is often connected with magic. Magic

widens the theme by connecting it with the irrational. Occasionally she includes too much black magic for the humanist reader to take seriously, as in *The Nice and the Good* (1968). Recently she has increased in subtlety: in *The Sea, The Sea* she contrasts two types of magic: that of the theatre director Charles, and paranormal powers learnt in the East by his cousin.

She sees magic as an aspect of religion, often equating it with spiritual powers: 'Buddhist cousin James is a truth-bearer. He learned paranormal powers in the East; which he now wishes to disown, to prepare himself for death.'[24] He suspects his powers, his demons, as he had killed the boy he loved in Nepal by attempting to warm him with his own body in the snow. By the end he forces himself out of his worldly attachments.[25] And Charles must learn, like Prospero 'to abjure his rough magic' and live with a more truthful view of himself and his influence.

Perhaps the most convincing inclusion of magic occurs when she equates it with psychotherapy in *The Good Apprentice* (1985). The psychiatrist Thomas admits his art is 'weak magic' compared with love or religion – 'God is a belief that at our deepest level we are known and loved.' (p.77) Thomas recognises that we must live without that belief, and attempts to heal by advocating life without myths or fantasies. He even recommends thinking about death: 'see it as a destruction of ego . . . liberation of the soul is the aim of true psychology . . . . It is from vain destructive wishes that death sets us free.' (p.257)

The young protagonist Stuart actually gives up research to devote himself to others – attracting much hate and anger. He is warned that selfless devotion cannot be achieved without taking account of sexuality, of the unconscious which is irrational, swayed by 'magic' forces. Thomas 'imagined himself coming to Stuart's rescue' (p.149). He is honest enough to recognise that he wishes to be a great healer, to canalise the unconscious: 'The dark powers are essentially ambiguous, thus enemies of morality. But I have to make benignant allies out of the most dangerous things in the world' (p.150). The altruistic Stuart, hoping to do social work, unleashes as much spite as good in others; to support his task he meditates without belief, a benign 'magic' that aids spiritual progress. Facing up to destructive and beneficent forces in our psyche is here grounded in a more satisfying intellectual way.

Murdoch differs from Plato in thinking that art must use some element of magic and enchantment before abjuring them. Certainly, the suspense and melodrama in her plotting stress the magic of story-telling. In *The Fire and The Sun* she suggests art is a vital element in helping us see more clearly; many of her characters have revelations of a better world while looking at a painting or hearing a piece of music: 'Good art which we love can seem holy and attending to it can seem like praying . . . for many in an unreligious age it provides their clearest experience of something grasped as separate and precious and beneficial' (p.76). In this, art is similar to love. Thus a saintly figure and an artist are often paired in her novels.

THE PURSUIT OF THE GOOD

Murdoch is unusual among modern novelists in appreciating our longing for the Good (and dramatising our inevitable failures) through convincingly moving characters, such as Michael in *The Bell* (1958). The pursuit of the Good is particularly well evoked in *Nuns and Soldiers* (1980), especially through Anne. Ten years earlier in *The Sovereignty of Good* she formulated many of her ethical ideas. She claims that the mind should be – and often is – directed towards concepts of the Good, of God, of death. She developed these themes in her Gifford lectures (1982), significantly titled 'Metaphysics as a Guide to Morals'. Here she emphasised notions of the Good already explored in her novels: 'Goodness is giving up power and acting negatively on the world' (*The Sea, The Sea*, p.445).

Both Yourcenar and Murdoch represent humans seeking to slough off some of the dross of ordinary living, to contemplate cosmic power. Many of their novels end with an experience of transcendence, a revelation of the value of the present moment. Both, like feminist theologians, turn from the male symbols of Judaeo-Christianity to less sexual symbols of ultimate reality. The novel of social quest has been enlarged into a novel of spiritual quest, in which the protagonist undertakes a journey whose purpose is to attain new spiritual knowledge. Few women novelists have tackled this visionary quest until Doris Lessing and Margaret Atwood in *Surfacing* (1979).

FEMININE SPIRITUALITY

In history, women have shown as great a spirituality as men, and the soul has traditionally been regarded as female. The many female mystics – Catherine of Siena, Teresa of Avila, Joan of Arc – prove the female capacity for intense faith. Murdoch admires the modern mystic Simone Weil, who shared intensely in the suffering of the hungry. Above all she admires Dame Julian of Norwich, whose famous 'All shall be well and all manner of thing shall be well' is quoted in every novel. Murdoch's novels, like Yourcenar's, support Lukács's contention that 'the novel is an epic of a world forsaken by God'.

Even if God does not exist, mystical experiences are gained by communion with Nature. Some of Murdoch's landscapes represent a mystical sense of Nature as source of heightened perception. This is defined as 'feminine' by the feminist critic, Moers.[26] Moers analyses landscapes of nineteenth- and twentieth-century women novelists and finds in writers like Willa Cather 'a sense of earthbound ecstasy, even physical dissolution, in a solitary, primordial land antecedent, even hostile to human life' (p.259). This might be a description of the rocks and mountain pool in *Nuns and Soldiers* in whose animistic presence two characters undergo transforming experiences. 'To look hard at Cather's landscapes is to perceive not the woman in the writer as much as the mystic' (p.260) – a phrase that applies to Murdoch's Norfolk landscapes in *The Good Apprentice* and *The Sea, The Sea*. In this novel the sea is both a frightening force – it kills the son, Titus – and beautiful – a momentary release from being. Moers provides the metaphor 'oceanic feelings' to describe the sensation of release from flesh to comprehension of Oneness. This can be achieved in the sensation of swimming, which Murdoch herself loves. Swimming in Kate Chopin's *The Awakening* and *The Philosopher's Pupil* expresses joy in assertion, in the physical, in neo-Freudian water images.

Murdoch's land and waterscapes are charged with symbolism and feeling, ranging from the personal to the mystical. Is the sense of mystery, even eroticism, pinpointed by Moers, female or androgynous? On reading *Tess of the d'Urbervilles* one is vibrantly aware of the lush valley where Tess falls in love, and the harsh hillside where she suffers alone. Hardy (like Murdoch) often interpreted his beloved landscapes in anthropomorphic and mystical terms. A close reading of some male landscapes might modify Moers' theory. But so far she has not been refuted. If the landscapes she analyses reflect 'feminine' sensibility in men as well as women, her study is not otiose, because she has highlighted attitudes which our society has undervalued, and are found strongly in women writers such as Emily Brontë, neglected till the twentieth century.

MURDOCH'S ATTITUDES TO FEMINISM

Murdoch has addressed feminism in various interviews. As early as 1962 when Hobson said, 'Surely you're exaggerating when you say that men are still trying to suppress women?' She answered: 'Oh no I don't. Look at *you*. You're trying to do it yourself.'[27] This comment shows her ahead of her time, understandable from the author of *The Flight from the Enchanter* (1956) where the depiction of ageing suffragettes is both wry and sympathetic.

To Biles in 1978 she spoke of herself as passionately in favour of women's liberation but qualified this by admitting, 'I identify more with men than women.' She added that she was not interested in the 'woman's world' or 'viewpoint' because 'we want to join the human race, not invent new separatism'.[28]

FEMININE AND MASCULINE ATTRIBUTES

Murdoch is unusual in preferring to inhabit a male psyche. She is particularly skilful at the first-person male narrator – generally a flawed character, forced painfully to face up to his limitations. There is a positive, almost instinctual love of writing as a man. Nevertheless she has pointed out that though male narrators may govern the text, there are female narrators within the text, especially in *Nuns and Soldiers*. There are female voices in the party gossip which often recounts events in her characters' lives. Indeed, it could be said that it is 'feminine' to extract the potential in gossip, psychologically and structurally. But on the whole, she like Yourcenar prefers the device of male narrator which enables them to use dominant cultural discourse, which they claim has not excluded them.

Murdoch's writing can be read as a 'double-voiced discourse' (Showalter's phrase describing women's ability to use patriarchal language and the muted female voice). If we pay less attention to the dominant plot, a female subtext emerges. This is notable in the imagery of *The Bell* (1958). The fruit-garden symbolises luscious yet enclosed, unfulfilled female sexuality, and Eve. The bell symbolises Dora's desire for self-assertion, and her learning not to 'play the witch'. A Dora-centred reading reveals a liberating feminism. *A Severed Head* (1961) contains the infrequent motif of a man yielding to a superior woman, armed with a sword capable of severing more than heads. The mysterious Honor Klein overcomes the wine-merchant Martin with her Japanese sword, symbol of power, intelligence and cruelty; the yin spirit stops the music and ends the pattern.

However the yin spirit seldom dominates. In the 1960s Murdoch's women were thwarted, cribbed, cabined and confined. The use of authorial devices such as male narration, multiple and elaborate plots, gothic settings and mythological patterns allows her to write of these experiences with control, even an odd detachment. This is partially accounted for by her 'feminine' unassertiveness, her reluctance to 'inhabit her action as fully as she might' (Byatt, p.204), based on an intellectual conviction that the author should be absent as far as possible.

She is unusual in her subordination of self, in omitting so much autobiography, even her harrowing work for UNRRA after the war. She prefers to impersonate, to create personae, or masks. *Under the Net* and *The Sea, The Sea* both stress the theatrical, in their imagery, in their treatment of illusion. Does she go too far in expunging self to impersonate a male? Does this prevent her from creating an outstanding character, in spite of her belief in the centrality of the individual?

We certainly notice the absence of a female voice as powerful as the many males. Nevertheless there is a plurality of voices in novels like *The Black Prince* which adds to the richness. Murdoch sometimes presents a disconcertingly ambivalent attitude to her female characters, making them small-scale, like Midge in *The Good Apprentice*. However, Ilona in that novel painfully learns independence, like Dora. Ilona and Dora might be described as the female text analysed by Cixous and Kristéva because they subvert patriarchal expectations by searching for *jouissance*, female pleasure. The opening out of plots after the 1960s has liberated some of her women. Her refusal of conclusions, in every other novel, testifies to the female capacity for change and renewal, showing women as 'subjects-in-the-making' in Kristéva's phrase. The three women in *Nuns and Soldiers* represent this, as do the two young girls in *The Good Apprentice*.

But apart from a few novels there is too little analysis of close female friendships, and feminists criticise the underplaying of women's relationships or women's community. Women are too often represented not working but falling in love, usually in a male-defined culture. It is significant that they are frequently presented from a male viewpoint, marginalised, undervalued. There are many 'silences' about female potential and intelligence. But to concentrate on these silences is of less interest to literature than to psychology since Murdoch is shrewd about her intentions. She gives the majority of her characters androgynous names, stressing the bisexuality in all human beings. These androgynous names, Julian, Hilary, Francis, Christian represent the potential for multiple identities and desires in all of us – and above all in their creator who refuses to be limited by gender.

MURDOCH ON WOMEN

As her novels have been well analysed by Byatt, Conradi and Dipple, I shall concentrate on three which show both increasingly successful formal experimentation and increasingly shrewd insights into women: *The Black Prince* (1973), *The Sea, The Sea* (1978, winner of the Booker Prize) and *Nuns and Soldiers* (1980.) (For a specifically feminist approach, consult Deborah Johnson, *Iris Murdoch*, Harvester, 1986.)

The Black Prince presents a searing picture of the suffering of rejected middle-aged women through the contrasted stories of the hero's sister Priscilla and the novelist's wife Rachel. They are both under-educated with successful husbands, who never reflect on a need to help them fill their lives. The repression of potential, the boredom of Victorian middle-class women, lives on in them, with its concomitant hatreds. Priscilla turns the hate against herself, like many Victorian heroines when abandoned, and commits suicide. Rachel has so much fire in her that she wreaks a sudden destructive vengeance on the men she has loved (worthy of a Fay Weldon persona). Bradley forgives her at the end: 'There must have been, to create such a great hate, a considerable degree of love' (p.383). Love was one of the few aspects of herself that society allowed a woman, and when that was spurned, consequences could be disastrous; usually for the woman at the end of many novels from the eighteenth to the twentieth century. Murdoch and Weldon in the 1970s show women suffering the age-old rejections, though some less humbly.

Murdoch universalises their predicament: 'Priscilla was a brave woman. She sat alone in the morning manicuring her nails while tears came into her eyes for her wasted life' (*BP*, p.82). Rachel 'stays at home and moves the furniture about and broods' (p.202), symbolising the desperate desire for change in someone limited to her house for self-expression. Priscilla, during her breakdown, calls insistently for her few jewels, the only objects left to her from a home taken over by her husband and his mistress; a pathetic identification with female adornment, when only a handful of objects is left of a lifetime's sorry home-making. Priscilla is shown at the most unbeautiful, obsessive stage of a nervous breakdown. 'Real misery cuts off all paths to itself,' comments her brother (p.135). He reacts with disgust to her heavy body and face ugly from crying, a neurotic disgust like Hamlet's for his mother's sexuality (p.78). Priscilla's suicide occurs at a moment which destroys the hero's love affair – an ironic comment on the effects of lack of brotherly affection. He finally admits that she died because not one person in the world managed to love her.

The first picture he gives us of Rachel is horribly similar to that of Priscilla – eyes puffy with weeping, words of hatred towards the husband who has misused them. His first comments on her subtly show the exterior view of a male who considers himself understanding: 'She was a good sort. One relied on her. One does not expect a woman to have ambition . . . . Women play blanker roles . . . in the play of life they have fewer good lines' (p.34). Her bedroom 'breathed the flat horror of genuine mortality, dull and spiritless and final' (p.38). This quietly shocking image gives the reader a foretaste of the end, which the imperceptive male narrator does not yet apprehend. Yet if he attended to Rachel's words he might. 'He has taken my whole life from me . . . . I am as clever as he is. All men despise all women really. All women fear all men really. Ask any poor woman in the slums. I shall never forgive him' (p.40). Rachel's experience links her with battered wives everywhere, in common physical humiliation.

Her husband, Arnold Baffin, a garrulous best-seller, has used incidents with Rachel for his novels. She understandably feels that he has left her no space. Like many male writers including Wordsworth, Shelley and Lawrence, he has appropriated female experience without giving credit. Arnold's own account of the quarrel is doubly shocking. First that she came towards the poker in his hand, then 'Every married person is a Jekyll and Hyde, they've got to be' (p.45). In this speech Murdoch reveals an Austen-like quality to allow the character to condemn himself through his own words: 'I suppose it's her age . . . I have to have women friends and talk to them freely . . . . Where it would make one mad with resentment one mustn't give way' (p.46). Of course, he had not allowed Rachel this freedom, he had not even allowed her to work, telling her she did not want to: 'It's a sort of empty complaint.' The arrogant assumption that he knows best how she should live her life is finally horribly punished with retributions almost as widespread as those in *Hamlet*, which inspires the title and many of the themes.

Gertrude and Ophelia were not asked what they think any more than Rachel and Priscilla are. Even when the brother is perceptive, it is with a touch of contempt, which the women resent. Priscilla bought

> horrible modern cutlery and an imitation bar. Even stupider vanities of the modern world have a sort of innocence, a sort of anchoring, steadying quality. They are poor substitutes for art, thought and holiness, but they are substitutes and perhaps some light may fall upon them. Housepride may have contributed, at times, towards the saving of my sister, towards the saving of many women. (p.83)

The daughter Julian might have an equally empty life if she had not chosen to write. Though twenty, Bradley only thinks of her as a little girl until he falls in love with her. His reverence and anguish are movingly depicted, so that we feel no repulsion at this obsession of an ageing man. Yet the fact remains that he did not 'see' her as a person until he saw her as a sex object.

THE SEA, THE SEA

In *The Sea, The Sea*, women who have been used and discarded slowly vindicate themselves. Rosina the actress taken from her husband comes back to 'haunt' the hero and punish him for the lonely abortion she suffered when he left. She later returns to her unhappy husband and she devotes the rest of her life to Northern Ireland, proving that Rosina possessed more devotion and selflessness than her self-absorbed lover had been aware of.

The dominant love story here is about obsession. The hero

tries to force his adolescent love, Hartley, to become what
he had once seen in her, to destroy what she really is –
an ordinary, lower middle-class housewife. There is no
condescension in Murdoch towards this dowdy, ageing,
unhappy mother. Indeed, we admire her when she shows
herself more mature than Charles. She wants to help her
unpleasant husband as 'no one else will redeem him, no one
else will love him' (p.301).

Charles sees himself as rescuing her, like Perseus and
Andromeda in Titian's painting in the National Gallery. Art
through the centuries has presented stereotypes that falsify
the individuality of women, encouraged men to see them in
a few inconographic representations, the virgin, the whore.
Hartley's moral triumph is to see the situation as it is without
fantasy that eventually proves destructive. This obsession also
proves an attack on romantic views of love as worship for its
own sake, that disregards the real woman. Charles, like
Proust in *La prisonnière*, exalts his ego and misuses another.
His prisoner becomes unkempt and dirty because he wished
to transform her into a 'phantom Helen' (p.174). He had
only been capable of loving a self-created image.

NUNS AND SOLDIERS

Nuns and Soldiers (1980) is unusual for her in that she enters
three female psyches. Not, as in *The Bell* or *Unofficial Rose*,
through just one individual but three, all of whom are
redeemed partially at the end. A greater compassion for the
complexities of women than she has hitherto displayed is
evident here: but it is empathy rather than mere sympathy,
as Murdoch begins unconsciously to share a feminist revaluation of women.

Gertrude presents elements of the grasping, middle-aged,
middle-class women of previous novels. She also echoes
certain qualities typical of the heroine of romance, finding
true love after misunderstandings. What redeems her is not
only the genuine mourning for her first husband, but her
capacity to give herself completely to Tim, an apparent
failure. By accepting the unsuccessful artist that he is, she
allows him to grow.

Murdoch makes us believe in Anne's vision, partly because she shares it, partly because it represents our longing for spiritual truth in spite of unbelief. In each novel at least one character aspires towards a mystical Good. Here she offers clues to both rational and supernatural explanations: respect for reason and the mysteriousness of human experience.

This 'nomadic, cosmic' (p.500) Christ continues to comfort Anne, in spite of her unspoken passion for the Count and her 'selfless, masochistic pursuit' of what she conceives as her duty, almost destroying Tim's marriage. (Murdoch does not fail to point out the destructiveness of puritanism.) Christ cannot solve her problems, but introduces a sense of universal spiritual longing.

The final chapter is devoted to Anne's realisation of her limits, her partial failure, her longing to lead a dedicated life. Anne is admired for her integrity, her selflessness, her pursuit of the Good. We have been movingly shown her inability to reveal her love to the Count. Anne chooses self-abnegating, life-denying service. Not happiness, but truth. She is the only one, apart from Guy, to learn from death: 'There are eternal partings . . . nothing could be more important than that. We live with death' (p.500). She then has a Murdochian revelation with which we are left: 'Goodness was too hard to seek and too hard to understand' (p.504). As she walks out into the snow she is rewarded with a vision of the sublime: 'It looked like the heavens spread out in glory, proclaiming the presence and the goodness of the Creator' (pp.504–5).

Ann Perronet in *An Unofficial Rose* (1962), had also pursued the Good, but with so many renunciations and negatives that she became 'deadening' to her husband. Dora in *The Bell* is a sympathetic portrait of a young, very ordinary woman trying to escape from herself and her environment. But neither is given the complexity or depth of the three women in *Nuns and Soldiers*. Anne is one of the most fully realised characters longing for Good. It is appropriate that she is a woman, since she incarnates the spiritual longing of many women, only recently emphasised in women's novels.

Daisy, the third central woman in *Nuns and Soldiers*, is an unproductive artist; she allows Murdoch to break out of the bourgeois milieu inhabited by most of the characters into the

world of seedy, insecure, dirty bedsitters. This sense of social
and economic isolation gives Daisy 'a strength of being which
others never touched or knew' (p.439). Daisy is one of her
best realised characters, with a quality of unexpectedness in
action and speech. Murdoch succeeds in endowing her with
the autonomy she longs to give all her characters. She and
Tim, her ex-lover 'counted themselves as wanderers, misfits,
mendicant artists. They prided themselves on being free.
They envisaged *soldiering* on . . . they conspired to be
eternally youthful.' This gently ironic self-image leads into a
subtle shift in authorial comment to indirect free style, to
catch Daisy's personality through her own words:

> She hated the bourgeoisie, the capitalist state, marriage, religion, God,
> materialism, anybody with any money . . . Heterosexual male humans
> were the nastiest animals on the planet. Some of them drove themselves
> literally mad with egoism. (p.71)

Murdoch amusingly represents the individual who cannot
distinguish (if such a distinction can justifiably be made) her
personal discontent from social criticism.

Her dialogue conveys Daisy's tone of voice delightfully:
'"Bloody baked beans again," said Daisy. "Fill my glass, dear
boy." Her haggard, handsome, thin face beamed.' The
rhythm of the three adjectives with their deflating end in
'thin' demonstrates what some critics underestimate, her
ability to write directly, tellingly.

Daisy's critique of Tim's paintings, and of those in the
National Gallery, widens the aesthetic context of the moral
debate.

> Painting is an image of the spiritual life; the painter really sees. At one
> time I wanted to be a painter. You see the world in a much more
> clarified way; important where one is thinking about other people,
> because they are the most difficult and complicated things[29]

claims Murdoch, linking some of Plato's ideas with her
novelistic 'realism'.

Tim's formal aesthetic structures represent Platonic ideas
of Form; Daisy, a failing painter, rejects the concept:
'Prettification, that's what your friends Titian and Veronese
and Botticelli are . . . take what's awful, dreadful, mean,

grim and disgusting and turn it into something pseudo-noble'
(p.129). Aesthetic dilemmas involve us because they are
grounded in conversation: Daisy's idiosyncratic voice underlines the problem of portraying evil adequately.

They have had this argument many times before, always
with Daisy pointing out that they are bad for each other.
Ironically, it is she, the more forceful character, who is
scrounging on Tim. Yet in the end, she has the courage to
make a new beginning for herself, putting her threats into
practice. The possibility of a new life for her as well as for
Gertrude and Anne, recognises the capacity of women to
survive: to display emotional and physical toughness, to assert
their value and to live by their own sense of what is Good.

THE PHILOSOPHER'S PUPIL

The Philosopher's Pupil (1982) moves away from London
Murdochland to a spa town where 'feminine' images of water
emphasise this versatile element. The philosopher is the aged,
brilliant, Rozanov, who returns from America to marry off
his granddaughter, Hattie. He rejects his now middle-aged
'pupil' George, whose venom reveals murderous instincts.
This novel is admired by A.S. Byatt for its study of violence.
I find it disappointing partly because the women are seen
from the outside, curiously stereotyped in nineteenth-century
mould. They are kept women – a ward, a widow, a mistress,
a frustrated housewife – all doomed by devoting too much
of themselves to one man (usually badly chosen) or frustrating
domesticity. They allow themselves to be exploited to boost
the egos of unsatisfied males. Murdoch illustrates the
destructive effects of male sadism and female masochism.
She concentrates on what it is like to live in hell, pursued
by self-constructed demons.

These demons recall both Dostoyevsky, whom she reveres,
and soap-opera. This could be an uneasy mix, but she is
prepared to take risks, to use the 'loose baggy monster' (H.
James' term for lengthy, nineteenth-century novels) to display
naked feeling. Her understanding of fantasy-realism is
intensely personal; she pursues error and expiation through

a first-person, somewhat fussy narrator, which nevertheless allows a melodramatic intensification of anguish. Rozanov is distraught at his inability to reach any truth, a frightening admission for a discipline often justified by a claim to pursue truth. A consolation male philosophers have found, faced with this predicament in the past, is to claim that their discourse is too difficult for women. Yet it is feminists who are pointing a way forward for philosophy with their constructive use of linguistic analysis. Their questioning of accepted meaning, of epistemology (central to philosophy) is based on moral concern for the opening up of this discourse to the experience of women. The marginalising of women in the novel suggests the waste of their capacity; this underpins, implicitly, the frustrated violence of the males, which might have been avoided by respect for the intelligence of women. Significantly, only young Tom, who respects Hattie as a person in her own right, is allowed happiness – and a future.

THE GOOD APPRENTICE

The Good Apprentice (1985) is more interesting, partly because the women possess greater vitality. The younger girls are prepared to take responsibility for their sex lives, even find work and earn a living. Gothic elements are amusingly exploited – an ugly, rambling, isolated mansion encloses an apparently devoted wife who preaches self-sufficiency while making dubious herbal potions. The half-parodied female gothic heightens the mystery, the foreboding, the realisation that good and evil are inextricably linked. Yet the close love–hate between mother and daughters is unexplored. Like male novelists, Murdoch leaves 'absences' about aspects of female relationships which do not interest her. She seldom examines female friendships because she foregrounds a frequent *human* inability to achieve the closeness and empathy demanded of real friendship.

She represents with increasing subtlety the difficulty of knowing other people. The characters here prove never to be what they first seem, while the complexities of their consciousness are skilfully dramatised. Murdoch leaves the ending and their futures as open as she can, in order not to impose patterns on them. Their ambiguity, our difficulty in judging are central. How far is the alternative lifestyle at Seegard fulfilling, how far is it destructive? Is Thomas the psychotherapist meddling or healing? Above all, is Stuart, the seeker after selfless Good, life-destroying or potentially constructive? Murdoch takes us inside the dilemmas of an idealist in the late twentieth century:

> If I can't communicate with people this isn't just innocent awkwardness it's a fault I must overcome, but overcome in my own way which I haven't found out yet. Am I giving way, daunted by being told I do nothing but harm? I haven't let myself take in that I've got to do it alone – I'm alone, but not in a romantic way. I may be condemned not to help people . . . I can't make sense of it. (pp. 445–6)

Stuart, like Thomas, is a 'good apprentice', longing to help others, yet horribly aware of our power to hurt those we care for most. Murdoch spends time searching for titles, and this unusual one symbolises a frustrated desire in most to achieve something better in their relationships than is allowed them by chance, genes, environment and lack of foresight.

CONCLUSION

After a brilliant clutch of novels in the 1950s, Murdoch's novels of the 1960s disappointed some of her admirers. However, since *An Accidental Man* (1971), the element in her fantasy has decreased, and the complexity of her moral analysis increased. By *The Bell* (1958) she had developed the mature structure for which she is celebrated, juxtaposing the orindary with the extraordinary, leaving the reader to decide which level of reality she most values. She dramatises the struggle between sexual and religious instincts, in the same world as Woolf, but with a less indulgent eye.

Her structures grow more complex, more satisfyingly open-ended, while her sympathy with half-failures deepens. She is improving in now combining pattern 'crystalline form' with 'chaotic stuff' of her beloved nineteenth-century novels. There are elements of philosophical fable – or rather moral fable –

fused with a real sense of the individual. Her experiments with pattern are increasingly subtle; *Nuns and Soldiers* opens and closes with a snowfall at Christmas; there is no incongruous element, such as the sea-monster in *The Sea, The Sea*. She consciously varies open and closed endings.

She is continuing with many previous elements, but a greater sense of possibility for individuals, and set against the awesome background of death. Her symbolism is becoming more complex in that every character in *Nuns and Soldiers* possesses some nun-like attributes, *and* has to soldier on. She is achieving the purposes she proclaimed for the novel in 1961 in 'Against Dryness': 'Literature has taken over some of the tasks formerly performed by philosophy. Literature can arm us against consolation and fantasy. But prose must recover its former glory.'[30] Her prose lacks the excitement of experimentalists, but often reaches from directness to eloquence. She has worked at the vocabulary needed for the unpretentious moral teaching of the nineteenth-century tradition which she has done so much to maintain alive and relevant. While developing a more positive view of society, she also emphasises the power of evil, shown in the violence analysed in *The Philosopher's Pupil* (1982).

Her admirers enjoy the paradox of seriousness combined with games-playing and ironic viewpoints. 'Good writing is full of surprises . . . . Good art is a pleasure which is uncontaminated, it's happiness. One also learns a lot from art: how to look at the world and to understand it; it makes everything more interesting.'[31]

Critical assessments of her work vary considerably. Dipple values her 'moral and ideological grasp of human failure' (*Work for the Spirit*, p.89). Conradi praises her as 'an original and powerfully intellectual theorist of fiction, an articulate and invigorating challenge to experimentalists', because she shows art as the instrument of knowledge. He coined the phrase 'Protestant romances' for her explorations of the difficulties of realism. One might call her stories philosophical fables (though she would reject the term) about the individual moral search in the puritan English tradition, since Bunyan. She stands out as defender of the now unfashionable concept of character. But are her characters varied enough, or are they too 'settled in bourgeois Oxford', as Kermode maintains? She cares a good deal theoretically about the individual, and makes fellow novelists rethink – as does her husband, John Bayley: 'modern impatience with the idea of character shows literary and moral failing.' Yet so far she has not succeeded in creating an outstanding twentieth-century character, like Bloom – or Molly.

Bradbury maintains that her practice often runs counter to her theories since she imposes patterns, while claiming that life has no pattern or meaning. Yet in her best novels she combines a sense of the mystery and formlessness of people's lives partly by intelligent use of concepts such as convention and neurosis – not as total patterning devices, but as instruments for the exploration of character and motive. In other novels, such as *The Philosopher's Pupil*, her inventiveness and moral concern conflict with her representation of individuals. Lorna Sage has coined the telling term 'aesthetic of imperfection' to account for Murdoch's sometimes conflicting aims and results. Sage sees Murdoch making exciting prose out of the very difficulties of writing today: 'The peculiar kind of illusion the books are after has to do with the deployment of a confident formula which stresses both the richness of detail and its disposability.'[32]

Certainly, Murdoch aims to bring back the richness of nineteenth-century rhetoric. Yet in spite of the diversity of voice in the narrative, some passages can be disappointing. At times her prose is not good partly because it harks back to a narrative form which was created in a society with different preoccupations. Interestingly, Murdoch considers writing threatened by theoreticians like Derrida, who would make language 'non-referential' – 'a terrible future'.

The feminist critic Deborah Johnson sums up:

Her distinctive presentation of characters in love is calculated to upset the usual Western vision of society as a hierarchy of relationships with the perfect couple at the top. In her relentless probing of the less acceptable areas of the psyche, of the various ways we lay waste our creative energies and of the power struggles which make up life in an aggressive society, Murdoch offers a surprisingly fresh and radical vision of the human struggle, both for self-definition and for connection with others. (*Key Writers*, 1986, p.132)

Dipple sees progress in the novels towards complexity and open-endedness, while A.N. Wilson considers *The Good Apprentice* her best novel so far.[33] Byatt paid tribute to Murdoch's moral and theoretical achievement, but concluded in 1965: 'she has not yet measured up to the size of her purpose. The inadequacies derive partly from the conflict between her own moral perceptiveness and her ability too rapidly to make patterns of great complexity with it' (p.216). That was twenty years ago. Since then, Todd [34] considers that she has improved by taking Shakespeare as her guide, because of 'his extraordinary ability to combine a marvellous pattern or myth with the expansion of characters as absolutely free persons, independent of each other'.[35] She possesses the power to structure significant images with cumulatively suggestive rhythms while recounting stories which represent ordinary mortals searching for love and moral values. And she has even more novels to write.

NOTES

1. From a talk given at Morley College, 20 October 1982. Extracts are published in 'Writers Talking', in *More* (Spring 1983).
2. 'Against Dryness', first published in *Encounter* (1961) and reprinted in M. Bradbury (ed.), *The Novel Today* (Fontana, 1977).
3. Interview with John Haffenden, *The Literary Review* (April 1983), pp.31–5.
4. Interview with A. Curtis, Radio 4, 8 August 1981.
5. Ibid.
6. See note 1 above.
7. 'An interview with Iris Murdoch', *Wisconsin Studies in Contemporary Literature*, 18 (1977), pp.129–40.
8. Gilbert Ryle, 'Jane Austen and the Moralists', *Oxford Review*, No. 1 (Hilary, 1966), pp.5–18.
9. In Deborah Johnson, *Iris Murdoch* (Harvester Press, 1986).
10. S. Gilbert and S. Gubar, *The Madwoman in the Attic* (Yale University Press, 1979).
11. See E. Abel (ed.), *Writing and Sexual Difference* (Harvester Press, 1972).
12. *The Good Apprentice*, p.251.
13. Abel (ed.), op. cit.
14. See note 1 above.
15. Ibid.

16. *The Sunday Times*, 29 September 1985.
17. Ibid.
18. 'Against Dryness', op. cit.
19. See note 1 above.
20. S. Freud, *Introductory Lectures in Psychoanalysis* (Hogarth Press, 1916–17).
21. See note 1 above.
22. See Freud, op cit.
23. *New French Feminisms* (Harvester Press, 1981), p.165.
24. See note 1 above.
25. 'I take a Buddhist view: it is difficult to overestimate the amount of illusion in any human soul. Art is to do with the clarification of illusion and movement towards reality' (Interview with Anthony Curtis, Radio 4, 8 August 1981).
26. Ellen Moers, *Literary Women* (New York: Women's Press, 1978), see Postlude.
27. 'Lunch with Iris Murdoch', *The Sunday Times*, 11 March 1962.
28. Peter Conradi, *Iris Murdoch: The Saint and the Artist* (Macmillan, 1986). This is a subtle and humanist analysis of Plato's influence on Murdoch.
29. 'Against Dryness', op. cit.
30. Ibid.
31. Ibid.
32. Lorna Sage, 'In pursuit of imperfection', *Critical Quarterly*, 19(2) (1977), pp.61–8.
33. A.N. Wilson, Review, *The Spectator*, 28 September 1986.
34. Richard Todd, *The Shakespearian Interest* (Vision, 1979). Includes a useful list of interviews.
35. *The Listener*, 4 April 1968.

BIBLIOGRAPHY

There are so many books and articles on Murdoch that I propose only the few which I found most interesting:
A.S. Byatt, *Degrees of Freedom* (Hogarth and Penguin, 1965), probably the closest to Murdoch's own views as they are friends.
Peter Conradi, *Iris Murdoch: The Saint and the Artist* (Macmillan 1986).
Elizabeth Dipple, *Iris Murdoch: Work for the Spirit* (Metheun, 1982).
   A comprehensive enthusiastic survey of all the novels to 1981.
Two brief introductions are:

British Council: A.S. Byatt and Richard Todd, *Iris Murdoch* (Methuen, 1984).

In the text *The Black Prince* is referred to frequently and is abbreviated to *BP*.

CHAPTER 2
A.S.Byatt
Fusing Tradition with Twentieth-Century Experimentation

Antonia Byatt is one of the most imaginative and intelligent writers of English today. She bears an affinity with Iris Murdoch, in that they are both writers of academic standing, who were established before the contemporary women's movement gathered momentum. Byatt devoted her first critical book to Murdoch (*Degrees of Freedom*, 1965), which considerably influenced her early writing as she was 'moved by Iris Murdoch's critical stand, her call for a large cast, her respect for the opaque individual'.[1] She shares Murdoch's concern 'to create real people *and* images'. However Byatt experiments far more with form – and above all with language.

From the late eighteenth century, women have played as great a role as men in shaping the novel in Britain. Fanny Burney, and of course Jane Austen, made it into one of the few genres where men and women could meet as equals. Sir Walter Scott admired the historical novels of Maria Edgeworth, and Jane Austen was held up as a model by influential critics like Lewes. Byatt points out that women writers in Britain have played a major role in creating our most significant types of novel.

Jane Austen developed the comic novel of manners, of social observation and shrewd moral judgement. The Brontës extended the gothic novel – virtually a female invention – to include a study of the subconscious, of dream, of women's spiritual needs. George Eliot developed the realist novel to discuss a wide range of contemporary philosophical, political and scientific ideas. Virginia Woolf developed twentieth-century impressionism, concepts of androgyny, modernism, freer structures. The fact that women were pre-eminent in these genres has given other women writers greater confidence in tackling a variety of novel forms.

'It does women a disservice to elevate them as women rather than writers because it prevents their being judged on merit. George Eliot is amazingly good on women, but amazingly good on other things as well.'[2] Byatt shares Eliot's wide-ranging interests, and like her, comments on contemporary critics, scientists, theologians and artists, to represent the moral *and* intellectual climate of their time. They are both interested in areas of knowledge which have traditionally been defined as the province of men. Their wide-ranging intellectual interests are infrequently commented on by feminist literary critics. Those in the Anglo-American tradition, led by Moers and Showalter, concentrate on novels where the heroine is repressed by society. Gilbert and Gubar are among the few to take on the challenge of analysing where fiction and culture limited Jane Austen and George Eliot.[3]

Nevertheless until recently, seldom have Jane Austen or George Eliot been studied as women, but claimed for the Great (male) Tradition. The over-influential Leavis coined the phrase 'The Great Tradition' for the title of his seminal book on those novelists he considered outstanding. In including Austen and Eliot in this tradition, male critics have performed a double-edged service. By highlighting their qualities as equal with male, they have taken them away from a women's tradition, which would have supported other female writers.

Ironically, feminist literary critics have done almost the same thing by neglecting these two novelists who show so little anger at their position in society. However, the imaginative approaches of French literary feminists led by Kristéva can include them. She celebrates the possibility of all people possessing 'feminine' and 'masculine' attributes, thus transcending the limitations of gender. Indeed Byatt considers the refusal to be bound by sexual identity releases creative energy in herself as a writer.

Byatt reads feminists, both Anglo-American and French, with more empathy than Murdoch: 'The feminist I most admire is Betty Friedan because *The Feminine Mystique* (1962) was written for my generation, who had been brainwashed into thinking that a woman's place, whatever her training and talents, was back in the home, bringing up children.'[4] She applauds the insights offered by feminists such as Moers and Showalter:

> I like both critics and Moers is very good on the female sexual landscape, though I'm sure I've encountered it as much in male writers. What frightens me is that I'm going to have my interest taken away by women who see literature as a source of interest in women. I don't need that. I'm interested in women anyway. Literature has always been my way out, my escape from the limits of being female. The writer's profession is one of the few where immense sexual-political battles don't have to be fought. There have not since the nineteenth century been deep prejudices against women writers.[5]

Feminists such as Dale Spender would not agree, since so many women writers of stature have been rediscovered only recently, thanks wholly to female publishing houses such as Virago. But Byatt, together with Murdoch and Lessing, refuses to be pushed into being a spokeswoman; like George Eliot, she is more interested in the origins of knowledge, the functioning of our brains, mental imagery and perception. Eliot felt free to incorporate ideas she discussed with Lewes after they had attended lectures on science and philosophy. Byatt feels free to quote from the ideas of Darwin, Einstein and Foucault when they illuminate her own thoughts.

Indeed, her recent novel *Still Life* (1985) 'is about knowledge itself'. Feminists point out that men have controlled knowledge, defining it frequently in ways which exclude women's experience. Though this may often be true, Byatt's enquiring mind has no inhibitions about garnering information on mental imagery from recent books including those by the mathematician Gödel, the psychologist Richard Gregory and the art critic Gombrich. Her pursuit of knowledge and the exact word denotes a scientific love of accuracy. Unfortunately, she is not interested in the feminists' claim that the very notion of what constitutes knowledge is male-defined. She is content to use the novel, like George Eliot, to discuss recent scientific theories. These two novelists attempt to rise above the divisions between the sexes, even the division between our two cultures, of scientists and non-scientists. To transcend divisions demands familiarity with the vocabulary of science as well as that of sensibility. Byatt's awareness of different discourses typifies the late twentieth century. She is a selfconscious novelist, brooding about the choice of words, meditating on theories about words.

Byatt is the only novelist in this study who admires George Eliot enough to imitate her: 'I started thinking about *The Virgin in the Garden* when a student asked why no-one could write a novel like *Middlemarch* now. I listed the elements we've lost: large numbers of characters, wide cultural relevance, complex language.'[6] Byatt shows these three elements are not lost, though she admits the uneasy relationship between the old form she has chosen and her newer preoccupations. In her critical writing, Byatt commented, 'the moral force of the Great Tradition still exerts its power, to produce forms sometimes limp, sometimes innovatory, sometimes paradoxical, occasionally achieved.'[7]

Her forms are never limp, but are sometimes overladen with cultural allusions that readers may not always find as 'culturally relevant' as she does. Byatt cannot take for granted the audience which Eliot, Dickens and Balzac knew awaited their work. She knows she cannot expect her own unusually wide reading in others, yet makes such frequent use of it that some readers feel alienated. *Still Life* faces the difficulties of realism today by sharing them with the reader. However the opening quotations from Van Gogh may fail to engage those who are less preoccupied with the problems of perception than Byatt. A few critics consider that she included too much of her wide reading.[8]

Yet if the novel represents our view of the world more than any other genre now, as many critics, from Lodge down to myself contend, then it is acceptable that Byatt includes scientific and cultural ideas which have transformed our thought. For her the novel is explicitly – not just implicitly – what Barthes defined as 'text': 'a multidimensional space in which a variety of writings, none of them original, blend and clash. The text is a tissue of quotations drawn from the innumerable centres of culture'.[9] Reading is a process of relating elements of text to centres of culture, to codes, to 'perspectives of citations' and 'the wake of what has already been seen, done and lived'.[10] Byatt helps us do this because she is unusually conscious of the many influences and codes she draws into her text. She works with the reader, using her knowledge of structuralism, not foregrounding it, but representing it through fully imagined characters in the tradition she admires.

Authorial intervention increases in *Still Life* to represent what the artist is thinking and attempting. From the earliest novels, such as *Don Quixote* and *Tristram Shandy*, we have the author talking directly to us, enjoying the irony of playing a character or even a critic of the work. Today many writers earn a living as critics, in journals or universities, and are shrewd in evaluating their own work. The double role of creator and critic in the one text appeals particularly. Byatt considers that a novelist who comments on the writing in order to alienate nevertheless only alienates during authorial intervention. On taking up the story, s/he can reassert the narrative pull, appeal again to the imagination as forcefully as Dickens, or fairytale. Byatt exploits this double discourse, she wants to make the reader trust the tale *and* the teller. How far does she succeed in the two modes, the apparent implausibility of the realist commenting on the creation of realism? Rachel Trickett considers that Byatt has not quite achieved the balance, that the imagined nineteenth-century characters predominate.[11]

Byatt herself gives equal weight to the metaphorical patterns and would like 'to include everything, like Proust'.[12] Proust is the twentieth-century novelist she most admires because he includes 'aesthetic, comic and horrifying comments in the same sentence'.[13] He can achieve many authorial discourses (ten narrative 'I's have been counted) but Byatt does not wish to make herself so central. Nor does she wish to write another novel about human relationships, in the tradition of Forster and Lawrence: 'When I'm describing love-making I'm not just interested in that couple, but in the genetic order of love-making.'[14] This leads to a quasi-scientific attitude: 'My characters are hypotheses let loose in the world, very like physiological or psychological experiments, with names and social backgrounds, to see how people react in test situations.'[15] Her discourse is experimental as well as traditional, shifting easily from the creative to the critical.

Until recently Byatt's reputation was based on her critical and scholarly work. She first made her name with *Degrees of Freedom* (1965) which remains one of the most perceptive studies of Murdoch's fiction. In 1970 *Wordsworth and Coleridge in Their Time* appeared, on two of the writers whose texts she interweaves into her own. Like her creation Stephanie, Byatt tried hard to think about *The Immortality Ode* when she was at home with small children. Some of her most insightful criticism is in scholarly articles such as 'People in Paper Houses' reprinted in *The Novel Today* (ed. Malcolm Bradbury, 1977). There she discusses the uneasy relationship between old and new forms in novelists she admires, including Doris Lessing and William Golding. Out of interest and to augment her income, she reviews for the *Times Literary Supplement* and Radio 3. She enjoyed teaching as it 'stops solipsism', but has accepted severance pay to devote herself to writing. She is currently working on a collection of short stories and a 'nineteenth-century type novel about the nature of history and evidence. Novelists like Balzac knew how complicated the world is. And he knew language is provisional. He also knew that it always had been immensely emotive *and* had described the world.'[16] Byatt typifies the novelist today, manipulating critical discourses in fiction and in academe.

It was while studying at Cambridge that she wrote most of the initial draft of her first novel. It represents an idealised and slightly mocking account of a god-like writer and an obsessive Cambridge critic, loosely based on Lawrence and Leavis. Leavis had a partially inhibiting influence as 'he did in a sense partly teach me to write by just looking at the way every word lay against the next word and made it seem that it was possible to look that closely. I write so slowly, with such complexity and with such perfectionism out of fear of Leavis.'[17]

Byatt's first novel, *Shadow of a Sun* (1964), analyses the shadow cast by a celebrated novelist on his adolescent daughter. The self-centred man enjoys remarkable visions which he explores in his writing – a theme she expands later.

Byatt takes a subject women excel at, the maturing of a young girl. Its end is modern and inconclusive, rejecting marriage for independence. Her second work, *The Game* (1967), is a skilful, harrowing short novel, welding nineteenth- and twentieth-century elements in form and theme. Through an account of a destructive sibling relationship she raises issues of good and evil, fantasy and fiction.

Byatt points out that the title evokes many ludic associations: 'gamesmanship, *homo ludens*, above all the shared literary game of the Brontës'.[18] Byatt half-parodies the creative apprenticeship of the Brontës. Her two sisters, Cassandra and Julia, are also brought up in Yorkshire and become writers. They play a game involving the invention of dramatic stores which feed the imagination to a point where neither can mature nor free herself of awareness of the other. This game exposes sexual, emotional and artistic rivalry. The two sisters represent differing attitudes to the novel: Cassandra the violent, self-generated imagination; Julia, the domestic observer.

Byatt edited George Eliot's *Mill on the Floss* and makes Cassandra, like Maggie Tulliver, allow her own death at the end. Both are so circumscribed by society that they turn hate against themselves, like many nineteenth-century heroines. Julia typifies the late twentieth century as she has a family and a job. Her writing is successful in expressing female dissatisfactions of the 1960s. Her naturalistic imagination feeds off her family, who feel preyed on, diminished by her fiction.

No genre before the novel has depended so much on realistic representation of people and relationships. 'Indeed the violation of private affection, the public exposure of someone else's suffering has become almost a rite of passage for male writers. However old-fashioned the interest women take in the ethics of the novelist, it is to the moral credit of Byatt, Drabble, Lessing and Murdoch that they continue to raise them.'[19]

Literature is a serious game, balancing between constructive imagining and destructive fantasy. The borderline is sometimes dangerously thin, as shown in *Madame Bovary* (1856) and *The Game*. Byatt offers a multilayered analysis of fantasy,

and its effects on love, religion and art today, including
television. Our idolising of TV personalities is subtly linked
with both the escapist dreams and the tormented dreams of
Cassandra, breaking under pressure. 'Identity under pressure
interests me most, as a novelist. What happens when a
personality slips into disintegration.'[20] Her characters fear
disintegration when the demands of differing personalities
threaten to destroy their development. She offers brilliant
insights into identity under pressure dealt with variously by
each character. Simon, the TV personality adored by both
sisters, escapes into the study of snakes; as herpetologist he
makes popular TV programmes where he can preach: 'Natural
selection is as immeasurably superior to man's feeble efforts
as the works of nature are to those of art'(p.257). This
Darwinism is fiercely opposed by Thor, Julia's Quaker
husband, because he longs to devote his life to a higher Good
than the nuclear family. Finally, he chooses to work in the
Congo, like Schweitzer. Thor's imagination is obsessed with
a desire to live his moral imperative of serving others. Byatt,
unlike Murdoch, recognises that this need not entail failure.
'He knows small acts are something in themselves. All the
rest of us are probably too conscious of our limitations'
(p.228).

The limitations, and potential, of the new medium of
television are skilfully discussed through a real situation.
Julia appears on a TV chat show that dramatises different
attitudes to the media and art. The producer claims that
television is 'the new art medium, other arts are too
compartmentalised' (p.185). No art form has ever wielded
such power as television, thanks to its immediacy. 'Television's
man's self-consciousness now . . . how many people see life
in terms of what the medium shows them?' This claim is
immediately contradicted. 'That sort of programme hopelessly
degrades art.' (p.185)

Postwar novelists have increasingly used the novel as a
vehicle to discuss art. Byatt widens the discussion by
comparing the artifice of camerawork to the needs of a
believer who transforms religious symbols into 'a tatty
substitute for glory' (p.146). The consolations of art and
religion are imaginatively necessary. But the terrible lesson

to be learned by the characters of Byatt and Murdoch is that they are partly imagined; we can only mature by ceasing to play games, by living 'alone'. Byatt has used this novel, like George Eliot in *The Mill on the Floss*, to grow imaginatively through limiting childhood affections to maturity as a novelist. They freed themselves to examine a far wider range of character and background.

THE VIRGIN IN THE GARDEN

Byatt took ten years to write *The Virgin in the Garden* (1978), one of the most impressive works of the 1970s. It is the first novel of a planned quartet, as ambitious as Lessing's *The Children of Violence* and Durrell's *Alexandria Quartet*. Byatt studies a group of characters during the second Elizabethan age, centring on the family of Bill Potter, a teacher in a minor public school. The emotional and intellectual development of his three offspring form the realistic basis of her study of the social and aesthetic changes of the whole epoch. 'My novels are about habits of thought and imagination: the quartet I am writing combines a partly parodic "realist" first and last volumes with a more experimental second and third.'[21]

The novel is set in a vividly depicted Yorkshire, where she grew up. Her powerful evocations of the English countryside help the traditional reader to accept the symbolism.

When I began *The Virgin in the Garden* I was studying seventeenth-century metaphor and narrative, and images relating to mind and matter. The world of the spirit and the fallen world of the senses. The subject developed through various Renaissance images of the virgin in a bower and Spenser's Garden of Adonis. Here the seeds lie quietly before they take on bodily form. I'm addicted to *The Faerie Queen* because of its narrative shape. He gallops, then suddenly freezes in order to read an allegorical meaning. I'd like the novel to do that.[22]

She has in fact enriched the realistic structure with Renaissance allegory, which in no way detracts from her realisation of character – a brilliant feat.

The plot focuses on the production of *Astraea*, a verse-play about the Virgin Queen, by Alexander, poet and English

master at Bill's school. 'It is a play within a play by a writer
who partially identifies with Elizabeth',[23] like Byatt herself.
The rehearsing takes place in a real Elizabethan garden, thus
momentarily linking the real present with a fictionalised past.
During the production, Alexander falls in love with Frederica,
Bill Potter's younger daughter, who enthusiastically plays the
young Queen. Their love symbolises the meeting of real and
imaginary, though it ends in frustration. In Alexander, Byatt
parodies the writer's passion for imaginary rather than real
love: 'He was a man of words. Once these were said, they
took hold of him' (p.333). Once he and Frederica have
spoken of love, they *will* themselves to believe in the power
of their words, while secretly preferring their imagined
worlds.

Alexander's play celebrates the wholeness of which Elizabeth is a symbol. 'In the *Virgin* I wanted to substitute a
female mythology for a male one. The male mythology is the
Dying God and Resurrection. The female one is birth and
Renaissance . . . I'm interested in . . . Renaissance because
things go on being born.'[24]

Byatt started with personal responses to her two chosen
periods, her youthful enthusiasm for the Festival of Britain
and for Renaisssance England. She agrees with T.S. Eliot
that language then was at its most alive and direct, because
'Donne feels his thought as immediately as the odour of a
rose.' Foucault, who has also influenced Byatt, proposed a
similar theory in *Les Mots et les choses* (Paris, 1966): that in
the sixteenth and seventeenth centuries there was no gap
between word and object, signifier and signified. However,
unlike T.S. Eliot she does not merely mourn the passing of
that apparently golden age of language, she examines our
many discourses today, and puts them in her text, in a rich
and complex web.

The Limits and the Power of Language

Part of her distinction lies in examining the limits and power
of language through narrative. Her multilayered approach is
illustrated in the account of the coronation of Queen Elizabeth
II. The modern icon-Queen is represented in diminutives
and superlatives, earnestly attempting to cope with Elizabeth's

'tiny figure' and the occasion. 'The Press used blandly lyrical, spasmodically archaic, uneasily hortative words about a New Elizabethan Age' (p.238). She includes discourse from newspapers: 'Churchill's rhetoric, heavy with worn and inherited rhythms'. She contrasts this with the unintentionally funny: 'might there not be something unseemly that a viewer could watch this solemn service with a cup of tea at his elbow?' (p.238).

Her characters widen the discussion; the poet Alexander declares later, on television, that they used 'flimsy vocabulary, trumped up, wilfully glistening sentiments' (p.241). Byatt gives Frederica, only seventeen, the freshest reaction. 'People had simply hoped, because the time was after the effort of war and the rigour of austerity, and the hope, despite spasmodic construction of pleasure gardens and festival halls, had alas, like Hamlet's despair, no objective correlative. But they had been naturally lyrical' (p.241). This is a clear example of the structuralist definition of text as an intertextual construct, i.e. the product of various cultural discourses. A 'text' consists of its ideological, political and psychoanalytical relationships with society and other texts. Some writers are unconscious of other discourses, as Barbara Cartland is unaware of cliché. But Byatt enjoys the intertextuality, the complex web created by interweaving from other texts, other discourses, other cultural associations.[25]

The two main words of the title of *The Virgin in the Garden* give birth to a complexity of cultural associations which transform the style into something rich and strange. The virgin is both Queen Elizabeth and young Frederica, icon and real virgin, powerful yet delicate.

Elizabeth Ist became my alter ego because she refused to marry. As a result she became the archetypal virgin, with power. She also assumed attributes of a fecund goddess, Astarte and Cybele, replacing the Virgin Mary in popular inconography. A paradoxical female figure began to rise in my mind, hermaphrodite as she 'hath both kinds in one' as was said by Spenser. This linked with my feeling (then, I'm more sceptical now) that an artist's mind should be androgynous, as Coleridge and Virginia Woolf believed.[26]

The garden of the title is the Elizabethan garden where

the play is produced, the garden of Eden and real and
symbolic gardens in and around the school. These gardens
represent both fertility and growth – and temptation in a
timeless place. The Master's walled garden is a pitiful modern
parody of a Tudor original; the Easter garden of the
Resurrection in Daniel's church contains only cut flowers.
The rugger field and biology 'bilge' pond represent the son
Marcus's inability to cope with expanses of nature until he
imposes mental lines over them. 'And there are parodies of
gardens – and corruptions of gardens of forms as in the
biology lab'.[27] Her gardens contain wild Elizabethan flowers
as well as cultivated flowers, reminding us of Ophelia's
symbolic flowers, and mad Lear crowning himself with
flowers – and recurrent flowering every spring. 'I want the
reader to stop and read the meaning of these gardens.'[28]

There are subtle schemes linking these frozen and living
images; they impose a poetic and intellectual unity on this
long work. Some readers dismiss them as 'intellectual
incrustation' but others, headed by the erudite Anthony
Burgess consider 'this is writing!'. Her writing draws on texts
she loves, lifting phrases to create this 'intertextuality'. The
result is often a brilliant new discourse, as in her description
of the butcher's shop window. She represents it in the
primary colours of the gardens: red, green and white; these
are also seen in Elizabeth's portraits, in Botticelli's *Primavera*
and quotations from Perdita's speech in *A Winter's Tale*.
With echoes from these texts Byatt creates an evocative visual
image for the disintegration of material objects, yet represented
in discourse which recalls Elizabeth David's joy in cooking
dead flesh, transforming it for one's children to eat. And it
is based on a real butcher's shop window which she used to
pass with her small children when she lived in Durham.
Byatt explains her method:

> All novels begin, like metaphors, when two things thought separate
> come together. I interweave things growing at one extreme, things cut
> and dying at the other. I was interested in the metamorphosis of one
> thing into another as I was involved in the mainstream of life with my
> small children. My characters are real and also metaphors. Daniel
> represents Dis, the god of the underworld. He is warm, dark, physically
> strong. He carries off Stephanie, who is seen in terms of whiteness,

passivity, feminine sensuality and spring flowers. She and Daniel form a unity.[29]

Metaphorical Language in Byatt

The Virgin in the Garden is rich in metaphor. *Still Life* on the contrary aims to use language as plainly as possible – even forgoes metaphor. Byatt found this almost impossible because most words do not merely denote objects, but are 'names, muddled metaphors, inventive, imprecise, denotative, practical, imagined'.[30] Apparently simple denotative words such as 'sunflower' contain metaphor. 'Words had been thought of as part of the thing they named. Later, men had become self-conscious, seen it as a web we wove to cover things we could only partially evoke or suggest. And metaphor, our perception of likeness, which seemed like understanding, could be simply a network of our attempted sense-making' (p.203). This structuralist comment from a Cambridge don in *Still Life* indicates the additional difficulties for a self-conscious writer today. Nevertheless Byatt here attempts a fascinating experiment: to pare down (where possible) to simple language in order to deal with universals which affect everyone – birth and death.

Metaphor in The Virgin in the Garden

Metaphor represents both an experience and an act, both the reception of a mental image and a deliberate act of understanding. It unites disparate elements. Disparate elements are united in the three pairs of lovers, who 'all have male and female in each of them'.[31] There are echoes here of Jung, whose analysis of *anima*, female qualities, and *animus*, the masculine principle, indicates that archetypal ideas of the opposite sex are present in all of us. We damage ourselves, like Lucas, when we destroy qualities of the opposite sex in ourselves which we may despise. Alexander is fortunate because he can identify with a literary tradition, and admire the carvings in Crowe's Elizabethan house, 'that hath both kinds in one', like the Queen herself. He also symbolises the possibility of androgyny in the artist. Besides, his 'primary impulses are not sexual, he's afraid of close contact. Such characters interest me. He's passive, responding

to events, unlike Frederica'.[32] Alexander adorns his room
with the reproduction of a beautiful hermaphrodite boy by
Picasso. 'He envies this boy who represents a frozen form of
what is eternally valid.'[33]

Byatt's use of metaphor recalls Derrida's comments on
Mallarmé's *Hymen*. 'The word "Hymen" is here a marriage
between desire and its accomplishment, a fusion that abolishes
contraries and also difference between. But hymen is also a
membrane, and a hymen between desire and its accomplishment, is precisely what keeps them separate. We have an
operation which brings about fusion and confusion between
opposites and stands between opposites, a double and
impossible operation'.[34] Byatt in her metaphors and Derrida
in his deconstruction are examining contradictions in our
discourse. Deconstruction accepts the distinction between
surface features of discourse and its underlying logic – and
illogicality. Metaphors give a clue to what is truly important.

Stephanie has a further metaphorical role as she is able to
use Romantic literature to interpret the world. For Stephanie
(and Byatt) literature illuminates mental concepts and articu-
lates spiritual longings. Byatt and many modern critics like
Derrida share what Nietzsche called 'the unshakeable faith
that thought, using the thread of logic, can penetrate the
deepest abysses of being'. They canalise their thought and
logic into literature: and for Byatt 'so much of art is
transmutation of memory'.[35] The memory of transforming
experiences from books (intertextuality) is as important as
personal memories.

We are at a late stage in our civilisation where many of
our ideas were formed by artists of earlier centuries. This
weight of tradition can prove inhibiting. Those who follow
tradition too closely lack a personal voice: experimentalists
who reject tradition may fail to gain adherents – as happened
with the *nouveau roman* in Britain. Byatt is too conscious of
the value of her culture to reject, instead she weaves it into
her text.[36] In so doing she is influenced by T.S. Eliot whose
fragments in *The Wasteland* 'shore us against ruin'. However
she differs from him in seeing not ruin but the potential of
the 1950s.

T.S. Eliot was subversive in using other texts to underline

the deterioration he sensed in his personal, public and cultural world. Byatt, perhaps because she is a woman, uses other texts to represent not only deterioration, but possibilities especially for her female characters. Her allusions are not to a dying but a revivifying culture. She interweaves fragments of seventeenth-century texts to represent twentieth-century girls because she *feels* their relevance in her own being. Of course, some allusions are a yardstick to measure the deterioration of the present, as in the comparison between the flowers in the Elizabethan garden and those in the modern parody of a Tudor walled garden.

However, usually she draws on our culture consciously and poetically to enrich the images and the analysis. A deconstructive critic also draws heavily on prior readings. In fact Derrida identifies various types of grafting of other texts: superposition, parallelism, analogy, coincidence. Byatt superposes many Elizabethan images in her description of Crowe's Tudor house, the setting of the play. Some critics object to the length of these, but I enjoy their aesthetic and saturnalian relevance. Byatt exploits another form of this when superimposing a long Proustian sentence (successfully) to describe the way memory enhances the past. At times she indulges in parallelism, echoing Wordsworth's *Prelude* to contrast with Marcus's unhappy experiences. Analogy and coincidence from poets she admires enhance the discourse.

These different types of intertextuality are also used by Joyce in *Ulysses*. Now that we have had long enough to appreciate his discourses we can accept his writing on many levels. It is not necessary to share his classical culture, although a knowledge of it enhances many episodes. *Ulysses* is vibrant because of the warmth of Bloom, the excitement of the language, the vitality of the Dublin streets. It is still possible today to fuse our cultural heritage into a twentieth-century vision of society, though more difficult for writers now than at the beginning of the century.

Byatt is acutely aware of what she is doing – a critical awareness developed by working concurrently on theoretical books: 'I think critical writing is a way of finding out how to write well. The gap between creative writers and critics has closed markedly in the last ten or twenty years.'[37]

The gap between her creative writing and her criticism of her own work is less than with most writers, which is why her own exegesis is so illuminating: 'The images in Alexander's play, blood and stone, flesh and grass, music and silence, the heard and the unheard melody, the red and white rose are the images of the novel.'[38] Byatt works with opposed images and experiences, life and death, animate and inanimate worlds. 'The novel came to me slowly while I studied the nature of seventeenth-century religious metaphor; and the development of narrative from Spenser to Milton, from allegory to epic. In all the works I studied there occurs the temptation of a virginal figure through the senses in a garden.'[39] All the main characters have virginal attributes and are tempted in various ways, fusing the metaphorical and the real.

Excitement with metaphor and with real individuals pervades her vision and her vocabulary. She is pithy yet suggestive, visual yet analytical, able to evoke landscapes and people, both for their own sakes and for their thematic significance.[40] One packed paragraph assesses a decade – or a minor character. One brief sentence throws light on the 1960s: 'they imitated anything and everything out of an unmanageable combination of aesthetic curiosity, mocking destructiveness and affectionate nostalgia' (p.10). She is acutely aware that she is dealing with the real world – but in a novel which is a language world. 'Language tries to capture and make permanent a moment in time which won't be captured.'[41] She draws the reader into her modern interest in the relationship between language and the world.

Each major character represents a different way of coping, or failing to cope, with the world through language. Stephanie and her father have different types of literary language; Daniel has the Bible, Alexander and Frederica try to dominate experience through their words, their education. The mad biology teacher Lucas muddles scientific and religious discourse, confusing himself and poor Marcus, who has no powers of language to protect him.

Byatt admires the passion and intelligence of the language of the seventeenth-century writers she studied and attempts to weave these aspects of their discourse into her text. She also catches a range of speech patterns from the intellectual to the simplistic: 'I hear their dialogues in my head, though I wish this happened even more.'[42] The conceited Cambridge undergraduate is disarmingly direct: 'I progress on all fronts. There's beginning to seem no point in actually getting a degree' (p.417). The pregnant schoolgirl: 'I feel green all the time. I don't enjoy anything any more, sex or champagne' (p.390). The bored, bawdy travelling salesman on his family: 'I sometimes feel I'm resented if I turn up, making trouble like, so I don't if I can help it any more, I don't put myself out dashing round, I send a nice postcard' (p.203). She catches with empathy and precision a range of discourse, both to allow the characters to speak for themselves and to further her discussion of ideas. These include a central issue, the difficulty of realism today. 'If we were in a novel it would appear suspect and doomed to sit here drily discussing literature,' comments Frederica to the English master she intends to seduce (p.349).

Humour

Such dry wit is an aspect of the levels of humour that lighten the work of reading. Byatt imparts her enjoyment of comic discourse through irony, literary jokes, moments of farce and the characters' own words. Frederica remarks hopefully, 'If you respect a scruple for a day or two, you get to feel you've done your duty to it, and hope necessity willl remove it' (p.352). Wit pinpoints both the minor characters and a whole decade. For instance, she mocks 1960s 'peripatetic folk with new ancient faces, variously uniformed, uniformly various' (p.12). She can be sardonic at the expense of the self-indulgent, as with Bill Potter, constantly losing his temper when others fail to be rational enough. (He is partly her mother, partly Leavis.) Byatt admits the influence of Murdoch's view, that the novel is essentially a comic form. The final sequences are a brilliant combination of farce with tragic moments, as the virginal couples pursue their desires, all to be frustrated by their own weaknesses.

Byatt manipulates farce sparingly. It represents crude reality intruding on illusion, but can prove a dangerous tool, descending to stereotype. This she avoids as each character has a tone of voice, an individual discourse. Furthermore, Byatt is skilled at presenting situational comedy: Jenny's attempts at adultery are constantly frustrated by her fretful baby Thomas, always crying at the wrong moment. Family quarrels are represented in all their destructiveness, yet make us laugh at their futility. She deliberately underplays the ludicrous in order to retain our sympathy for all the characters.

Black comedy mounts towards the end of *The Virgin in the Garden*, underlining our absurdity even at moments of greatest mental misery. The virginal Lucas attempts to castrate himself while the virginal Frederica pursues her half-reluctant prey. Byatt's innovation is to introduce the perspective of Elizabethan saturnalia into black comedy. As in *A Midsummer Night's Dream*, the saturnalian structure turns the expected courtship patterns upside down: virgins woo, experienced males are nonplussed; the night and Nature seem to possess aphrodisiac forces freeing lusts. The novel is at its most saturnalian just before the terrifying climax, as two women hotly pursue Alexander, while first Lucas, then Marcus break down.

The comedy finally turns into tragedy; hers is a tragicomic vision in which we are frustrated by our own weaknesses, failures in perception and unavoidable limitations. Byatt presents a complex view of humanity where few can live with themselves, though some are represented arduously, or comically learning.

Two Male Writers who Influenced Byatt: Twentieth-Century Novelist Proust and Romantic Poet Wordsworth
Above all twentieth-century novelists she admires Proust as 'his book is his life and his life was his book'. Though *The Virgin in the Garden* is not autobiographical, she resembles Proust in including crucial elements from her own life. She and Frederica were both seventeen in 1953; she and Marcus both suffer from asthma and migraines; and she acted the Lady in Milton's *Comus* in Trinity Hall garden.

'I know I echo Proust'[43] – echoes can be heard in sentence-structure and treatment of time. She shares his use of the novel to speculate on consciousness, on death; and on the impossibility of fully knowing another person, partly because of the changes caused by time. They both use language to attempt to make permanent moments in time 'which won't be captured'.[44]

Proust provides another way of seeing time, he looks backwards and forwards, like Byatt, from a present they are partially in and partially outside. Time (and art) help humans not only define themselves, but create. Byatt gives us glimpses of Proustian *mémoire involontaire* as Frederica and others look back. However, the *mémoire involontaire* that he gained while tasting the madeleine comes no longer involuntarily, but through metaphors reviving disparate, distant moments in time.

Her characters exist mainly in a present which is now past – 1953, the year of the coronation. However, they look back on it from the vantage point of the Prologue, placed in the 1960s. Furthermore, the novel is written in the 1970s, recalling Elizabethan England. This represents a golden age, not unlike Frederica's memories of the play. What is real at the moment of experience nevertheless needs the shape imposed on it later by memory.

All the characters embody aspects of her own attempt to grasp a sense of the real – and forms to embody reality. 'Marcus is like me in being asthmatic and having moments of arrested vision when things stop and the light is too bright. I used to defend myself by geometry, like him. What I was trying to do is difficult: to create someone for whom the world comes unmediated. He can do instant mathematics by imagining the problem being worked out in a garden, without explanation – just like a friend of mine.'[45] 'Geometry was close to, and opposed to, the suffering animal. It intensified with pain, and yet the attention could, with effort, be deflected from pain to geometry' (p.91).

Marcus is first presented to us alone, on the rugger field which 'lay about him in his infancy' (p.27) – a phrase deliberately quoted from Wordsworth. Furthermore, Marcus's visions are described like those of the child Wordsworth in *The Prelude*, as 'spreading'. But unlike Wordsworth he does not feel privileged when he 'spreads himself'. He has elements of the child-seer, but bereft of religious blessing. Through him Byatt is testing the literary and psychological

legacy of Romanticism, its exalting of the child's vision. But
in a world without religion Marcus can only undergo, without
illumination. 'The light was busy; it could be seen gathering,
running, increasing along the lines where it had first been
manifest. Wild and linear . . . ' (p.120). His visions, unlike
Saint Paul's (or Wordsworth's), cannot be used. They are
shown only from his point of view, with no authorial
endorsement. 'Without diminishing the magnitude of Marcus's experiences, Byatt removes from them all associations
of traditional privileged glory.'[46] He is completely isolated,
from family, friendship, even understanding. 'He dislikes his
literary family. He has no language to mediate his visions.
Thus he is vulnerable to the forms of language which protect
other characters.'[47]

Her study of the inadequacy of some modern discourse is
taken further in the pseudo-scientific vocabulary of Lucas,
the biology teacher who befriends Marcus in order to use his
visionary powers. He claims, not unlike Teilhard de Chardin,
that 'the Goal of Existence is the transference of Material
Energy into Mental Energy' (p.147). Lucas hopes to use
Marcus for this, but what they transfer telepathically is
pitifully unilluminating – a few patterns merely.

His language is a pitiful parody of the Bible and science,
from which he has learnt almost nothing. He is 'virginal' in
being so untouched by knowledge which he debases by a
farcical misuse of conceptual language.[48] His vocabulary is
religious, biological, mythical, psychical. Marcus has no
linguistic defence against Lucas's explanations of his visions:
'Photisms. Experiences of floods of light and glory which
frequently accompany moments of revelation. The phenomenon of course is open to scientific doubt . . . You could run
away now but God would engineer another nasty shock'
(p.125).

When Lucas breaks down, Marcus is left 'on his own with
things which initially had been almost too much for him'
(p.340). Thus he follows Lucas into hospital, where he
becomes delirious, then silent. His end is left uncertain,
though we guess that he might recover slightly in the sequel.

Rather than being a wisdom figure like Wordsworth's child, Marcus
embodies terrors and loneliness inseparable from the condition of not
knowing oneself . . . . This is a most realistic and most equivocal

treatment of the visionary child . . . It is the terror and pity of childhood, rather than its serene wisdom that interest Byatt.[49]

Terror and pity for the man alone is harrowingly portrayed through Lucas. He longs to make contact with the noosphere and[50] with Marcus, but fails at both. His loathing for his unfulfilled homosexuality is linked with his mental collapse when he goes 'archetypally mad' (p.395). In his horrifying breakdown he becomes 'the thing itself, unaccommodated man'. Such echoes from *King Lear* begin on the second page where Londoners are 'accommodated and unaccommodated', thus suggesting, as in tragedy, that something terrible will occur. It does, with Lucas's attempted self-castration, the virgin's hatred of the burden of desire. Through Lucas she presents a detailed, tragic study of a mind and body unable to cope with pressures; a study informed by knowledge of post-Freudian psychology. Is there also a parody of the compulsive pattern-making of the modern novelist? 'Lucas goes mad because he fails to keep images separate from each other.'[51] He attempts to be too schematic, not unlike Byatt. But she realises that his image-making cannot cope with his reality. She admits irreducible reality in the senselessness of suffering.

Women in The Virgin in the Garden

The increasing freedoms of the late twentieth century allow Byatt to study a wide range of women from the most intellectual to the least assertive. She has the authority to describe ordinary women's lives since she has shared them as wife and mother. She can include the frustrations of the graduate at home with a baby and the grief of a bereaved parent since she has experienced both areas of existence. But her aims are wider: to continue the nineteenth-century search for fictional heroines who combine strength and intelligence with 'feminine' qualities. Nineteenth-century classical education represented a dividing line between men and women. Dorothea felt excluded, whereas Frederica insists on sharing. Woolf admired the way Eliot's heroines nevertheless reach 'beyond the complexity of womanhood and pluck the strange bright fruits of art and knowledge'. Neither Eliot nor Byatt had to sacrifice authenticity and self-exploration nor accept the dominant culture's definitions as binding.

Byatt is unusual in approaching the concept of virginity, which she studies on many levels, and in all her main characters, male as well as female. They are presided over by the Virgin Queen, who encouraged iconographers to use her emblem to replace the potent, fecund Virgin Mary. The Virgin Queen is powerful because of her separateness admired by both Alexander and Byatt, who often expresses herself through him. Virginity gives power, yet involves limitation: it represents a burden which Frederica and Lucas long to lose; both are tempted in gardens, like metaphorical figures of virginal purity from Spenser to Milton.

Most nineteenth-century heroines are virgins, requiring time to be wooed and won. This gave a pattern to the plot, which the fast bedding of the post-pill generation has undermined. Byatt has replaced the traditional pattern of courtship with the saturnalian pattern of *A Midsummer Night's Dream* (which aided Murdoch in the structuring of *The Sacred and Profane Love Machine*, 1974). Characters pursue and are pursued, frequently at the wrong time and by the wrong person. The male desire to deflower the virgins acting in the play is shown sympathetically, as are the unfortunate consequences for the young girls.

The first woman described is significantly the Virgin Queen Elizabeth I, one of our greatest statesmen. Her likeness in the National Portrait Gallery displays 'the doublenessess that went beyond the obvious ones of woman and ruler . . . young and arrogant . . . knowing and distant' (p.13). These attributes are mirrored in different ways in all the women, especially Frederica. Elizabeth was 'a figure whose over-abundant energy attracts dubiously mixed emotions, idolatry and iconoclasm, love and fear, and the accompanying need to reduce and diminish their strangeness and ordinariness' (p.13). Thus Elizabeth was transmuted into myth, differing with the opinion of the viewer; she was seen as whore, as clandestine mother, as a man, even as Shakespeare! Before feminist critics appeared, Byatt was analysing the potent images of virgin mother that circumscribe, describe, distort and mythologise both ordinary and extraordinary women.

There is implicit feminism in the exploration of female iconography, but no polemicism. Indeed, few English writers have adopted the vocabulary of radical feminism, except Angela Carter and Fay Weldon. Many prefer evolution to the invention of a language free of gender distinction. 'I like change, not revolution. I like subtle distinctions with a continuing language, not doctrinaire violations,'[52] Byatt wrote in 1975; nevertheless she resembles Lessing in forging new images for women. And both show anger, frustration and sexual drive as motive forces as strong in women as in men. Showalter comments: 'For the first time anger and sexuality are accepted not only as attributes of realistic characters but also as sources of female creative power' (p.35).

The double critical standard of the nineteenth-century prevented women from using passionate or technical vocabulary to explain their feelings. Thus in *Middlemarch* Dorothea's frustration caused by her unconsummated marriage can only be dimly adumbrated. Byatt does not suffer from this restriction. She gives practical insights into female reactions to lovemaking which show how much Mary McCarthy's *The Group* (1963) encouraged the imparting of useful detailed knowledge. An almost feminist extolling of female biology transforms the language after Stephanie's satisfactory wedding-night: 'Her perpetually glittering and perpetually renewed inner spaces, black-red, red-black, flexible and shifting with no apparent limits . . . a sunless sea, brimming with its own shining white blowing sand, with a night sky just beyond vision' (p.282).

Stephanie, Bill Potter's elder daughter, although clever, suffers from passivity inherited from her mother. Byatt conceives her partially through images of whiteness, like Persephone, to be awakened by love. Her surprise at falling in love, her fear of loss of intellectual life are movingly fleshed out. She forms part of a schematic pattern as she interprets the world to herself and her students through the romantic language of Keats' *Ode on a Grecian Urn*. Yet she is a convincing individual, finding new life in the release of energy through marriage to a good man, Daniel; he realises her capacity to care for others – when not left to her virginal separateness.

Her lack of forcefulness comes from her mother, Winifred. Through a thumbnail portrait as incisive as Murdoch's, Byatt explains her morally, sociologically and genetically. Furthermore, we suffer with her as she is buffeted by Bill's angers and ambitions. 'She was afraid of living like her mother, too many children, too little money, mastered by a house and husband which were peremptory moral imperatives and steady physical wreckers. Winifred had been her mother's confidante about every detail of blood, polish and indignation . . . ' (p.86). The moral comment of the omniscient narrator is sparingly but incisively used. Winifred's misery as she witnesses the gradual breakdown of her silent son adds to the survey of humans under stress.

This is counterbalanced by the portrait of Jenny, the peevish, unfulfilled, graduate wife. Her longing for fulfilment through adultery is seen somewhat externally, to add to the increasing sexual farce. In the hands of Edna O'Brien or Drabble she would have been the angry protagonist. Here she is both individualised in her suburban house, and pitied as her fractious baby ruins her nights and attempts at seduction. She is torn between love and hate for her teething, tyrannical child, infuriated by her desire for the poet Alexander, who prefers to express himself through words, rather than actions. She makes us aware of further aspects of sexuality, inhibitions and misplaced affections, while her unconsummated pursuit of Alexander increases the saturnalian comedy.

The central virgin is Frederica, only seventeen, representing an angry intellectual separateness. The intellectual adolescent is shown as trying to grasp the world through books when she falls in love. 'It was in clichés that Frederica had discovered, invented, fantasised, constructed, read and written him, so: ascetic, saturnine, a little harsh, melancholy, black-browed. . .' (p.201). There is only limited language available to the girl to describe her feelings, paralleled by the paucity of models for women.

Byatt indicates that sexism in language is not simply *man-made*: it is a wider reflection of the power-balance in our society, where until recently men have done most of the *naming*.[53] Frederica had no idea what it was to be a woman;

nor had she many ideas to help her understand men. 'The composite knight of Frederica's early myths was put together out of floating cultural clichés' (p.208). There follows a fascinating sequence where Byatt takes a much wider view of all the influences on a girl's psyche when she falls in love. She includes the sociological, the psychoanalytical, the physical, the aesthetic and the mythic. Byatt gives to her young heroine discourses (also recommended by feminist critics) so often in the past only granted to heroes. The narrator's breadth of discourses overcomes the stereotyped language of the young woman. It also overcomes some of the limitations of heroines who discover the world sexually rather than through work or spiritual quest.

In *Still Life*, Frederica symbolises the modern woman who enjoys her sexuality, her intelligence, her education and her power. She reveals the capacity of women to be the equal of men in these spheres. Byatt proves, more convincingly than Woolf, the capacity of the artist to apprehend male and female attributes within complex characters. The refusal to be bound by sexual identity releases creative energy. Byatt excitingly transcends many arguments about gender difference. A suitable representative of the second Elizabethan age because she achieves equality in diversity.

An Historical Novel

Like *Middlemarch*, *The Virgin in the Garden* can be considered an historical novel. *Middlemarch* encompasses social change at the time of the 1832 Reform Bill; it represents an epoch and its effects on a community. *The Virgin in the Garden* compares the first and second Elizabethan ages. Byatt states wryly:

> I thought I had a perspective on time in the early sixties, with young children growing. It seemed a long time since I'd left school in 1953. Now I see that's absurd, but I wanted to write a historical novel. The Coronation allowed the comparison with Elizabeth the first and the metaphor of her life. I wish I had more feeling for social patterns, because I certainly wanted to say something about English society.[54]

Byatt presents what many readers demand – a perspective on their society. She represents changes in social attitudes from the long-suffering mother Winifred, brought up in poverty before the war, to her fiery daughter Frederica, insistent on a full emotional and intellectual life. In Alexander she traces changes in writing from verse-drama to prosaic commentaries on television. Vignettes of groups, authorial comment and a wide spectrum of fairly representative characters, from the wealthy entrepreneur Crowe to the footloose travelling salesman, recreate the 1950s. She feels a special fondness for the 1950s in their hardworking, liberating, tawdry diversity.

Women have frequently chosen to write historical novels. In the eighteenth century those of Maria Edgeworth and Clara Reeve were praised by Sir Walter Scott. The twentieth-century has seen many women prepared for the hard labour of research before inventing plot, from Marjorie Bowen, admired by Graham Greene, to Helen Waddell, a worthy forebear of Byatt in her combination of scholarship with emotional insight. Marguerite Yourcenar represents the widest aim, surveying scientific and philosophical thought in the Renaissance, and in Hadrian's Europe. Byatt is less ambitious, she interweaves her wide reading of Renaissance texts and her own experience.

Conclusion to The Virgin in the Garden

Byatt displays the ability of those in the 'Great Tradition' to structure a large cast in many differing situations within thematic and poetic patterning. This patterning aids the exploration of good and evil, right and wrong, conscience and emotion. These concepts are embodied in remarkably fleshed-out characters. Indeed, both reveal an unusual capacity to make even the minor characters live (such as Bulstrode in *Middlemarch*; Bill in *The Virgin in the Garden*). These are viewed sympathetically and sociologically yet possess autonomy. And Eliot and Byatt have the rare quality of depicting goodness. Not failures in pursuit of good, as in Murdoch, but hard-working men who try to live their ideals, like *Adam Bede* (1859) and Daniel, the curate in *The Virgin in the Garden*. In Dickens and Balzac, the hardworking man of goodwill remained in the background. Byatt, like Camus in *The Plague* (1947), foregrounds a secular saint, giving us a humanist vocabulary to discuss vital moral issues.

STILL LIFE (1985)

In *Still Life* (the second of the quartet) she ironically presents criticisms of her (and Murdoch's) approach. 'Art can't be thought of as inventing people and giving them names and social backgrounds and amassing descriptions of clothes and houses' (p.215). So declares Cambridge don Raphael Faber, who admires French writing and the anonymity of Mallarmé. Faber is narcissistic, but his poems have some value and there is uncomfortable truth in some of his pronouncements: 'Van Gogh lacks selflessness . . . in the post-Christian world he hasn't come to terms with' (p.315).

Still Life is a *tour de force*, but more direct in style, with the aim of capturing 'the thing itself' like a painter. She attempts the almost impossible: to depict 'the illuminated material world' (p.2). Things become stunningly alive, plums, a French beach, a tree, like images by Van Gogh. She explores the complexities of naming and of accuracy by quoting from Van Gogh's letters and commenting on his painting. 'Metaphor lay coiled in the very name sunflower, which not only turned towards, but resembled the sun, the source of light' (p.2).

She has succeeded in reducing her use of metaphor, but like Van Gogh realises that even the simple word sunflower suggests rich meanings. 'Metaphor, our perception of likeness . . . a network of our attempted sense-making' (p.203). In our process of naming we build pictures, even metaphors. Yet, 'I had the idea of a novel of . . . naming the multitudinous things to be seen for the sake of seeing them more clearly' (p.301). And she does make us see more clearly. For instance a black carving is 'image and bones, altar and woman, half-doll, half-idol, the thing itself' (p.82).

She admits that 'our infinite apprehension is trapped in corruptible and limited flesh' (p.286) and shows her different characters struggling to express their perceptions. Stephanie, now a devoted, overworked mother, suffers because she

cannot use all the words she knows to her beloved son.
Alexander, writing a play on Van Gogh has trouble in finding
an appropriate language for the painter's unmediated colour,
his obsession with the visual world.

Byatt stated in a recent article:

> I wanted to write about birth and about death and sex. I decided to
> try to write a novel which should be as plain as possible – a novel
> eschewing myths and cultural resonances – a novel which would try to
> forgo metaphor . . . . I wanted my thoughts, my descriptions, to move
> between simply *naming* like Proust's 'clear and usual' images, and the
> kind of mental icons which are the Sunflowers. Colour was one of the
> most powerful movements from the purely descriptive, to Van Gogh's
> idea of the world as battleground between the complementary colours,
> which he said he painted as the marriage between lovers.[55]

Like Proust, she distinguishes between metaphoric names,
invested with life by his imagination, and simple words,
which present a clear, usual image, like a child's object-
picture of a bird or a chair. Proust's phrase 'Les mots nous
présentent des choses une petite image clairc et usuelle' is a
foreword to her text. A better translation is possibly 'Words
present a clear *commonplace* image of things'.

This attempt to use clear, usual words shows a belief that
words denote things: that accuracy of description is possible
and valuable. She wishes to resist the fashionable idea that
reality is a 'bounded world bearing only the shape of our
imagination'. She even gives a list of the interestingly named
grasses which Marcus studies for 'A' level because 'these
names stand to me for the relation of words to things,
inventive, imprecise, denotative, practical, imagined'.[56] Byatt
is trying to let things speak for themselves. *Still Life* is a
mistress-piece capturing real objects as well as real people. She
has achieved a kind of reality that has seldom been novelised
in this way before, so giving a new lease of life to realism in
the modern novel. Facts themselves resonate with real-life
narrative. Like Van Gogh painting olive trees, there is both
passion in their observation – and simple reality.

The simple reality of the ageing parents living in Yorkshire
is one of the strengths of this novel. Winifred and Bill go
through the rejection by their three children to find a portion
of happiness in their grandchildren, empathetically depicted.

Like both Proust and Arnold Bennett Byatt celebrates 'ordinary things and everyday life'. Some of the best passages describe universal experiences of birth and death, married life and bringing up small children. Male critics find the description of Stephanie giving birth (after harrowing waits in ante-natal clinics) provide fascinating insights into women's experience.[57] Byatt's analysis of the rich complexity of simple words links with her vision of the rich complexity of ordinary lives.

Ordinary experience enriches the narrative, with particular empathy for women. 'Winifred has recently realised that there was something in being a woman, a mother, in late, tiring middle age that automatically alarmed and irritated others. She seemed to herself swollen and grotesque, dead hair, dull eyes, numb' (p.147). Byatt is particularly moved by Winifred because of 'her capacity for giving up. It's also a weakness, she retreats too easily'.[58]

It is her two daughters' experiences that are the most absorbing. The demanding Frederica explores the world and men while worrying 'if it was possible to make something of one's life and be a woman' (p.184). Her intellectual experiences at Cambridge involve us in discussion of the process of novel-writing today and the links between fiction and reality. 'Whereas she recognised the humilations of Lucy Snowe and the death of the heart, she failed to recognise the professional coquettes of pure young girls of male novels' (p.129).

Such muted feminist criticism is seen in a wide context: 'the loving interest lavished on all female activity, all female uses of the self is the most agreeable result of literary feminism' (p.184). Loving interest is lavished on Stephanie and her experiences of motherhood. Byatt evokes both her frustration at the small amount of words needed by a housewife, and her satisfactions with growing things. We share her humourous observation of her toddler. 'Will grew, stretched, changed shape. He stood with wavering hands and jack-knifing knees . . . . She thought she would never forget any of these moments and forgot them all as the next stage seemed to be William and eternal' (p.226).

Through Stephanie's loving, self-abnegating relationships we have one of the best modern descriptions of a good

marriage. Byatt set herself the demanding task of encompass-
ing not only birth and marriage but death. She possesses the
power to disturb in the meaningless tragedy of Stephanie's
accidental death. From the outset Byatt had intended to
include the accidental, which here is appalling. The resulting
suffering and grief are movingly conveyed through character.
The husband Daniel can scarcely cope with such loss:
'ordinary words, like stones, turned live Stephanie into
remembered Stephanie . . . . He had not begun to know that
she would not come again . . . . He began to move things,
folding her clothes away . . . . Howl he told himself . . . go
on howl. He could not' (pp.338–9). This powerful novel ends
abruptly, with the pointless inevitability of loss, the almost
wordless suffering of the individual.

CONCERN WITH RECENT THEORIES ABOUT LANGUAGE

Since the structuralists began writing in France we have been
made to recognise the gap which exists between a word and
the object or thought to which it should adhere in the
mysterious act of naming. Feminists such as Dale Spender
have been influenced by structuralist examination of 'gaps'
between words and thoughts. She points out in *Man Made
Language* (1980) that many words do not convey women's
experience, but men's, and that words such as doctor,
solicitor, politician create images of white males – images
which exclude women and blacks. This examination of
patriarchal 'gaps' in language has been a fruitful spin-
off from structuralism, frequently without its theoretical
underpinning. What interests Byatt is the theory and the gap
between signifier and signified in the much wider sense of
the gap between our mental images, our words and the
world. She perceives language as limited by our means of
apprehending the world, not just our gender. In *Still Life*
she quotes Van Gogh in analysis of the problem of conveying
sensory perception in two dimensions – or words. She takes
the dilemma of conveying colour, unconnected to gender.
She spends pages showing how difficult it is for language to

conjure up the richly subtle purple sheen of a plum. She questions how far this experience of purple comes to us unmediated, which for her would be like living in paradise, or how far we need the mediation of the words – or paintings – of others to help us 'see'. Her colour images are powerful means of attempting to depict 'the thing itself'; they also lead from the purely descriptive to Van Gogh's idea of the world as battleground between or achieved resting-place of, the complementary colours. Significantly, he claimed he painted these as a 'marriage between lovers'. In pigment, through colour, he was aiming, like Byatt, at dreamed union: an occasional overcoming of a modern sense of disjunction.

Byatt's language in *Still Life* succeeds at times in overcoming a modern sense of disjunction. But she intends to concentrate on the disjunction between intention and words in the third projected novel *Evidence*. 'It moves on to some kind of linguistic crack-up, to the gap between private and public language.'[59]

Eliot and Byatt have both been criticised for their authorial intrusions. Both use them, not to intrude as characters in their own right (unlike the male Sterne) but to comment omnisciently on the impossibility of omniscience. A sensitive reading of the narrator, like Professor Barbara Hardy's, reveals a subtle swinging from omniscience to indirect free style, voicing the characters' thoughts. But as narrators, they delight readers by pinpointing affinities between science and literature. Byatt quotes revealingly from Einstein: 'Human nature has always tried to form for itself a simple and synoptic image of the surrounding world. It tries to construct a picture of what the mind sees in nature. All these activities are reconciled by acts of symbolisation' (p.275). Byatt maintains that literature, language, science, indeed the human mind suffer from the same longing for order, and difficulty in achieving it. This interest in science enriches her comments on heredity, mind, everyday behaviour and sex. 'I realise I am following George Eliot in feeling it right to include many aspects of modern knowledge.'[60]

Amongst other scientists, both have read Darwin. Byatt quotes from him to stress her feeling that a dual process occurs in novel-writing and in nature, a combination of 'the

accidental and the formed'.[61] She explains this in *Still Life*:
'Darwin tried not to personify the force that chooses egg-cell
and sperm . . . . But where do we stop thinking about chance
and choice, force and freedom? We cannot resist the
comparing and connecting habits of mind' (pp.235-6). The
comparisons – and oppositions – define, redefine and modify
their characters, their perceptions and the structuring. 'To
find form, not impose it.'[62] Both see 'the novel as a way of
coming to terms, of mapping the world' (*The Times*, 22 June
1985). While describing a little boy trying to walk she
observes: 'Human cognition is a patterning of the world with
a constructed map crystallised in genes, repeating laws already
informing the growing mind' (p.237).

CONCLUSION

The world she maps is vast, from prehistory to modern
physics. She speculates on Platonic and Freudian myth 'that
the hermaphrodite came before the constructions and cell-
divisions of Eros – an impossible stasis, a world without
desire?' (p.179). Here she is even using the symbolism of
her title *Still Life* to suggest a possible asexual golden age.
Like many modern artists she is disturbed by Einstein's
Theory of Relativity, but studies him to put it into perspective:
'There would be no theory of relativity without the absolute,
immutable idea of velocity of light. We can't have the idea
of random happenings without simultaneously a concept of
order, of form, of law' (p.178). She possesses double vision,
theoretical (often thought male) and practical, a using of
experience.

Byatt combines fictiveness and realism brilliantly. Like
Eliot in *Daniel Deronda* (1876), she includes many aspects of
modern knowledge, which she researches assiduously. Yet
both are equally interested in their young, suffering, learning
heroines. That novel is often introduced to the public through
the Gwendolen Harleth episodes. Such treatment would turn
The Virgin in the Garden and *Still Life* into bestsellers, because
the central story is gripping: the Potter family, with irascible
father, obsessed son and two daughters discovering the world

and their sexuality. Eliot and Byatt write for adults with empathy, intelligence, humour, seriousness and passion which place women firmly in the great tradition.

NOTES

1. Talk with Rachel Trickett, Radio 3, June 1985.
2. Talk at Morley College, February 1985.
3. S. Gilbert and S. Gubar, *The Madwoman in the Attic* (Yale University Press, 1979).
4. Janet Todd, *Women Writers Talking* (New York: Holmes and Meier, 1983). pp.181–95.
5. Ibid.
6. See note 2 above.
7. From a conversation with Byatt, February 1986.
8. e.g. Peter Kemp, *The Sunday Times*, 30 June 1985.
9. Roland Barthes, *Image, Music, Text* (New York: 1977), p.148.
10. op. cit., p.28.
11. See note 1 above.
12. Ibid.
13. Ibid.
14. Ibid.
15. From a discussion on the experimental novel, Radio 3, 5 July 1986.
16. *Times Higher Educational Supplement*, 2 June 1986, p.3.
17. Ibid.
18. See note 2 above.
19. Elaine Showalter, *A Literature of their Own* (Virago, 1978), p.316.
20. See note 2 above.
21. Todd, op. cit.
22. See note 2 above.
23. Ibid.
24. Todd, op. cit.
25. For more on intertextuality see J. Culler, *On Deconstruction* (Routledge, 1983).
26. See note 2 above.
27. Ibid.
28. Ibid.
29. Ibid.
30. From 'Les mots et les choses', written for a symposium held at Westfield College, February 1986, p.17.
31. See note 2 above.
32. Ibid.
33. Ibid.
34. Jacques Derrida, *La Dissemination* (Paris: 1972), p.212.
35. See note 2 above.

36. She distinguishes between 'greedy reading' and 'parody' in 'People in Paper Houses', in M. Bradbury (ed.), *The Novel Today* (1977).
37. Todd, op. cit.
38. See note 2 above.
39. Ibid.
40. Each page is enriched by authorial reflections: 'Pain hardens, and great pain hardens greatly, whatever the comforters may say' (p.383).
41. J. Dusinberre, 'Forms of reality' in A.S. Byatt, *The Virgin in the Garden', Critique*, vol. 24, no. 1 (1982), pp.55–60.
42. See note 2 above.
43. Todd, op. cit.
44. Ibid.
45. See note 2 above.
46. Judith Plotz, 'A modern "seer blest": The visionary child in A.S. Byatt's *The Virgin in the Garden'*, PMLA (1980).
47. See note 2 above.
48. 'Lucas has attempted to rewrite the book of Genesis in modern scientific language and makes both seem a total farce. He has debased both the religious tradition in which he grew up *and* scientific curiosity' (see note 2 above).
49. Showalter, op. cit., p.316.
50. In discussion in Critics Forum, Radio 3, September 1985. For a succinct account of iconography, see Lisa Jardine, *Still Harping on Daughters* (Harvester Press, 1983), pp.169–79.
51. See note 2 above.
52. See note 15 above.
53. See also D. Cameron, *Feminism and Linguistic Theory* (Macmillan, 1985).
54. See note 7 above.
55. See note 15 above.
56. Ibid.
57. See note 50 above.
58. See note 2 above.
59. Ibid.
60. Ibid.
61. Ibid.
62. Ibid.

CHAPTER 3
Margaret Drabble
Foregrounding the Female

Margaret Drabble began writing in the early 1960s when she rapidly achieved success. Her novels emphasised tensions in a woman's existence created by the desire to live a full life while caring for children to whom she is devoted. Her particular innovation lay in the depiction of educated heroines whose preoccupations reflected those of her middle-class readers. Drabble differs from other women writing of their predicament in her highlighting of maternity. She compassionately portrays its complexities: the absorbing quality of maternal love, coupled with its inevitable, limiting anxieties.

She initiates a making public of women's private emotional conflicts. Yet 'none of my books is about feminism because my belief in the necessity of justice for women (which they don't get at the moment) is so basic that I never think of using it as a subject. It is part of a whole.'[1] This desire for justice suffuses her whole structure. She shows how a woman's life is restricted by her own and society's attitude to her. Her first novel, *A Summer Birdcage* (1963), charts self-discovery and painful rivalry. Subsequent heroines are frequently inhibited sexually; they cannot give their bodies easily in love but to their surprise find fulfilment in child-bearing. Their discoveries of their reactions as women shape the plots.

Jane, in *The Waterfall* (1969), sees the forces acting on 'our bodies as unwilled, as foreordained as the sliding of mountains, the tidal waves of the sea' (p.182). This is virtually a rewriting of Freud's dictum 'Anatomy is destiny' and in images suggestive of female sexuality. With the insights of feminist literary criticism one sees Drabble is writing out of her body, her sexuality.

Ironically, Drabble began writing for similar reasons to many Victorian women novelists – she was lonely, bored, jobless, middle-class. Of course, with forebears such as Jane Austen there is no need to feel ashamed of the pursuit: furthermore, she concedes a university education had given her a sense of the validity of her own opinions. Nevertheless, she wrote about the risks of falling in love and having babies because that was what she knew, and what constrained her. Drabble recommends that young writers should begin with their own experiences, as the capacity to analyse other minds is rare.

The Garrick Year, completed in 1964, and *The Millstone* were both written during the enforced introspection of pregnancy. Her fourth novel, *Jerusalem The Golden* (1967) won her critical approbation which has increased with every subsequent novel. *The Waterfall* (1969) has been made into a successful television serial, a tribute to its dramatic qualities.

DRABBLE THE CRITIC

Drabble, mother of three, supports herself by her writing. She also works as critic in the media where she is shrewd and reliable. She has written various critical studies, including *Virginia Woolf: A Personal Debt* (1973). Her best is probably *Arnold Bennett: A Biography* (1974). As hard-working as Bennett himself, she researched the early journalism and what he learnt from editing a woman's magazine; she describes his heavy working day, his travel, his financial affairs. She regrets not travelling to America ('because of small children') to look at his papers there, but has nevertheless produced a readable, scholarly work on a novelist she loves.

In 1979 she produced *A Writer's Britain: Landscape in Literature*. This is the first book to combine images of different regions and periods into an analysis of the ways writers have changed our visual attitudes, our taste in landscape, and our relation to nature. She points out that the Romantics gave us the idea of nature as a powerful spiritual force which has

influenced so many writers, including herself in early novels.
She comments perceptively: 'Hardy observed the smallest
details of soil, contour, crop and vegetation, and he adds to
this an antiquarian interest in topography, and a poet's use
of language: his ear was as keen as his eye, and he could
hear the wind whispering in the harebells, and tell each tree
from the distinct rustling of its leaves.' She includes urban
landscapes in this study and in her later novels, reflecting
the experience of many readers. Indeed in her hands the
novel is a record of contemporary life, a record almost as
reliable as a sociological survey.

PARALLELS WITH WOMEN SOCIOLOGISTS

It is instructive to note the parallels with sociologists, Hannah
Gavron's *The Captive Wife* (1966) and Betty Friedan's *The
Feminine Mystique*. Both questioned the prescribed roles for
women by asking women about their lives. All three suffering
from isolation with children, wondered why they could not
conform to the public image of devoted wife and fulfilled
mother. 'There was a strange discrepancy between the reality
of our lives as women and the image to which we were trying
to conform.'[2] Friedan, Gavron and Drabble raised some of
the issues to preoccupy society and lead to politicisation of
feminism.

Drabble draws on a rich literary tradition, Friedan on
sociology and Gavron on interviews. Yet all used women's
experience as their starting point, in order to explain it. Such
personal involvement characterises much feminist research;
it indirectly criticises the right of men to encode knowledge
about women.

To their surprise they discovered they had a good story
when they exposed what the official version on women
concealed. They knew women were expected to be happy,
yet experienced disappointment bordering on despair. Many
were made to feel at fault, neurotic, since no credibility was
given to their problems. 'When a woman tries to put the
problem into words, she often merely describes the daily life
she leads' (p.27). Friedan revealed a tight-lipped suburban

scene, like Janet's in Drabble's *Realms of Gold*. The misery
of the housewife's daily routine which Friedan named the
feminine mystique was later named as an aspect of women's
oppression by Sheila Rowbotham, and many others. Friedan
and Drabble and Gavron (and Nell Dunn with *Poor Cow*)
were among the first in the 1960s to show the oppressiveness
of the role of 'housewife-heroine' which denied them a life
of their own. They opened the door on women's experience,
to focus on its galling features: the paradox that when
education was beginning to emancipate women (male) psychol-
ogists constricted them to the full-time socialisation of
children.

DRABBLE'S EARLY WORK

The early novels follow her own development, though she
claims they are not autobiographical. However, they reflect
the preoccupations of a woman of her own age, from marriage
and divorce to lovers and remarriage. They display an
increasing skill to organise plot and sketch character while
touching on important themes.

She depicts female subjectivity deriving from women's
physiology and bodily instincts. These bodily instincts, such
as fear of sexuality in *The Millstone*, affect the unconscious;
and it is the unconscious which moulds the way her heroines
envision their possibilities and attract experience. She draws
from her own life to reflect the experience of many other
women – which accounts for her popularity. She analyses
female lack of confidence *and* how much is learned from
having children. More than any other writer of the early
1960s she divorces sexuality from maternity. For her the
great discovery of self comes through the complex reactions
of being a mother.

Drabble does not draw the sharp distinction made by
later feminists between 'female' which implies biology, and
'feminine' which implies a cultural construct. She merely
glimpses what is problematic in the term 'maternal instinct',
but leaves it for the women's liberation movement to make
this subject explicit.[3] She does not question how far women's

desire to have babies and maternal love are 'innate' or 'constructs'. In *A Summer Bird-Cage* Drabble was not consciously feminist. 'But', she says, 'I discovered that many women were going through identical experiences. It expresses my astonishment that the freedom to work *and* have babies led to the complete exhaustion of being two people at once. The recognition of this problem has taken away some of the burden of guilt. There are undercurrents of rage, but those are veiled protests compared to the eighties.'[4] Her achievement is to highlight the tensions raised by her enjoyment of motherhood and her resentment against the oppressive role of housewife. She does not politicise this issue, but by juxtaposing these two themes, leaves the reader to reflect on the mother's role in patriarchal society.

Womanhood – particularly maternal knowledge – has been extolled by French theorists such as Hélène Cixous. She claims a close link between female bodily drives (pulsions) and the act of writing: 'Bodily drives are our strength, and among them is gestation drive – just like the desire to write: a desire to live self from within, a desire for the swollen belly, for language, for blood.'[5]

Menstrual blood was mentioned with joy by Drabble first. It becomes a symbol of wholeness at the end of *The Waterfall*. She caused a stir when she talked sanely about her view in 'Words' on Radio 4 at the time. In bravely publicising her healthy reactions, she prepared the way for books such as *Wise Wound* by Shuttle and Redgrove (1980), which highlights the creative aspects of the menstrual cycle: Lessing, in *The Golden Notebook* (1962), had mentioned the discomfort of a period; thus breaking the patriarchal taboo and allowing women to communicate more freely.

Indeed, *The Golden Notebook* and Drabble's early books coincided with several novels by youngish women talking from a specifically female standpoint. The finest is Lessing's as she links the roles of writer, mistress and mother in an imaginatively experimental form. Lessing's wide-ranging assault on masculine values spearheaded this emerging biology-oriented feminism, to be consolidated politically in the late 1960s. One of the most notorious novels then was Mary McCarthy's *The Group* (1963). She initiated frank descriptions of contraception and women's sexual responses. She made as powerful a metaphor of the (contraceptive) Dutch cap as *Moby Dick* had done for the whale. Edna O'Brien's *The Country Girls* (1962) expressed a fierce, high-spirited longing for more than society would allow women: enjoyment and sexual freedom. Sylvia Plath, in *The Bell Jar* (1963), voiced the longings that had been awakened and left unsatisfied. While in *The Pumpkin Eater* (1962) Penelope Mortimer foregrounded gynaecology – a hysterectomy and its psychological effects.

'There is no point in sneering at women writers for writing of problems of sexual behaviour, of maternity, of gynaecology. Those who feel the need to do it are actively engaged in creating a new pattern, a new blueprint. This area of personal relationships verges constantly on the political,' Drabble told the National Book League in 1973, with the benefit of hindsight.[6]

THE PURITAN INHERITANCE

Another topic which engages her is the inherited puritan conscience, its strengths and weaknesses. It offers relief in hard work, but teaches emotional and sexual inhibitions that must be struggled against, especially when the pill was radicalising attitudes to sex and marriage. Drabble argues that the moralistic conscience should be transcended by charity, and love of their children transforms her heroines: in the early novels they are marked by a combination of sexual frigidity and maternal passion that creates conflicts bordering on depression. Of *The Waterfall* she states, 'It was about the painfully depressive side I wanted to write – also the fear of complete abandonment which sometimes goes with exteme passivity.'[7]

Her heroines are not usually passive: rather, they are torn by the conflict born of following their instincts for survival through love, against the moral code their parents had imposed (however gently) upon them. The constraining effects of nurture and its spectral but real pressures on adults trying to find their own way is a theme linking all her novels,

as they progress to the problems of middle age. The early
novels are underpinned by expansive use of Biblical words:
sin, salvation, vice, soul, suffering, sacrifice, martyrdom:
lending symbolic weight to the recognition that there is no
solution to the conflict between instinct and morality.

Once her three children were at school, Drabble was able
to open her world. She 'could afford the time to go by bus
to the lawcourts' to study the background to her one male
protagonist in *The Needle's Eye*, Simon. Here the puritan
preoccupation widens to examine the possibility of living on
the material minimum in our secular society. The lonely
individual soul is analysed in increasing depth against the
background of money-making, strikes, union law-breaking,
even the corruption of an African country (to which the rich
heroine Rose gives all her money in an attempt to save her
soul – hence the title). Drabble is aware of the puritan danger
of shattering the self by subservience to the will. Rose, like
all her heroines, has to mature slowly, but survives by
remaining capable of loving and forgiving.

The Needle's Eye is one of her maturest books. The heroine
Rose attempts to live on her own, and in a poor area, thus
moving away from patriarchy's definition of what is important.
She creates a new space for herself and her children, without
her husband. Her efforts recall the words of Mary Daly, the
feminist theologian: 'The process of liberation involves the
creation of new space, in which women are free to become
who we are, in which there are real and significant alternatives
to the prefabricated identities provided within the enclosed
spaces of patriarchal institutions.'[8]

For many readers there may be too much religious
symbolism. 'It is sacrifices that God has always demanded
. . . it's the only way to find him,' states Rose. Yet through
sacrifice Rose achieves a step towards integration, thus
implicitly criticising male ego-centredness.

Male characters are often shadowy, albeit sympathetic
figures in Drabble's early novels. George, the father of the
illegitimate child in *The Millstone*, is respected as having an
important centre of being, yet he is not told of the existence
of his child. Drabble realises women writers are frequently
judged on their ability to depict men. She has shown

increasing insights at this and in Simon, the lawyer in *The Needle's Eye* she represents a self-doubting, conscientious man, unhappily married, tenderly in love with Rose.

Drabble's criticism of patriarchy is understated. Nevertheless it is implicit in the detailed account of the unfeeling treatment of women in ante-natal clinics, in the indifference of doctors and the lack of sympathy of most of her male characters to mothers' feelings. Brought up as a Quaker, Drabble exempts patriarchal religion from feminist scrutiny. Indeed, her religious imagery shows a conviction that this is an area which men and women share.

Since the 1970s she has experienced less inhibition in writing about men. Her view is not unlike that of Deborah Cameron who believes that neither those who posit a man-made language nor the anti-humanists provide an adequate explanation of the partial alienation of women. 'Since language is a flexible and renewable resource, and since girls must come to grips with it as their socialisation proceeds, there is no reason in principle why language cannot express the experience of women to the same extent that it expresses the experience of men.'[9]

Ironically, in using private knowledge of women's lives, Drabble has provided a social documentary on our time. This marks the beginning of the making public of women's intimate experiences. Far more than Murdoch and a little more than Byatt, she uses the novel as a vehicle to show us how we live. In this she is similar to Anglo-American feminist literary critics. They read novels for information about women's lives and feelings. Toril Moi criticises this 'Images of Women' approach for 'not recognising the "literariness' of literature, for tending towards a dangerous anti-intellectualism, for being excessively naive about the relationship between author and text.'[10] Nevertheless by charting lives similar to her own, from adolescence to middle age, Drabble bears witness to increasing awareness, increasing confidence. She now suggests possible autonomy, admittedly in heroines lucky enough to be talented and educated – and seldom poor. She expresses new pride in women's knowledge and difference, at the end of *The Millstone* and in Frances of *Realms of Gold*. Frances provides a new role for women. She is successful at

her profession, a loving mother and finally able to find a
mate she can respect as well as love. At forty she is a survivor,
with women's warmth and what had hitherto been considered
men's work. Drabble herself is not unlike Frances in that
she has achieved a happy second marriage and variety in her
work through the editing of the *Oxford Companion to
Literature*.

As the early works are sensitively examined in *Puritanism
and Permissiveness* by Valerie Grosvenor-Myer (1974), I shall
concentrate here on *Realms of Gold* for its character studies
and *Middle Ground* as a post-realist social survey. Drabble
demonstrates the flexibility of the traditional novel by
narrating open-ended stories while keeping a partial plot,
suspense, portraiture and social comment. Her gentle feminism helped to prepare the ground for the more sardonic
women writers of the 1980s.

THE REALMS OF GOLD

The preoccupation with the pervasiveness of the puritan ethic
is sloughed off almost completely in *The Realms of Gold*
(1975). Her

> many layers of intentions were not wholly fulfilled while writing. I
> intended a family saga, based on three cousins who had not met before.
> This would enable me to examine three sections of English life, three
> biologically different personalities, against a background of social
> mobility and genetics. I did a great deal of research on geology and
> volcanoes for the cousin David, but as I wrote Frances began to take
> over.[11]

This reflects her method: a partial plot evolves in her head
while she researches necessary areas. During writing (about
a year and a half for each novel) different characters or
themes surface: as with Russell Hoban it is sometimes only
half-way through that the final form begins to emerge. The
writing of the second half may then become less arduous
than for novelists who plan every detail in advance. Hopefully,
the resulting form 'is a crystallisation of the sense of validity
of what I am saying'. Frequently, the form emerges through
the emotional development of the protagonist, in earlier

works through unhappiness, now through success, to a recognition of the possibilities for happiness.

Realms of Gold takes its title from a quotation from Keats' 'On first looking into Chapman's Homer': 'Much have I travelled in the realms of gold.' Frances, an archaelogist, unearths a lost city, which contains gold bars, not just broken pots. Drabble intended an analogy with the creative process which, like archaeology, depends on a combination of chance and choice: 'These worlds of the imagination exist and can be entered.' The title underlines certain symbolic intentions that first appeared in *The Garrick Year*, which stressed the symbols of water, drowning and the Garden of Eden. 'Realms of Gold' are the sands of the Sahara where Frances achieves fame from expeditions and conferences and realises her potential for leading a rich life.

Drabble comments: 'At this point I felt I could take off and describe someone whose life was much broader than mine. I deliberately made Frances much travelled as I wanted to describe different places. Increasingly, I was able to give lecture tours and reflect wider panoramas, which was immensely exciting'.[12] This sense of excitement and optimism is personified in the warm, productive, middle-aged heroine, and enriches the lives of the two cousins she meets in adulthood.

The geologist cousin David diminished in importance as the writing progressed, but he is given some of the most optimistic social comments: 'He held the minority view that the world's resources are more or less illimitable and also self-renewing.' He experiences a sense of continuous creation when he visits the Hebrides: 'The landscape seemed alive, as though seething in the act of its own creation, for round every island the waves broke white and fell and glittered in a perpetual swell . . . . Out they stretched forever, to the ultimate reaches of man's desiring.' This description of creation stands out in Drabble's writing as one of the few to include sexual imagery which here enriches her discourse.

However, the sense of breadth given by geological evolution narrows when Drabble considers the evolution of the central family, the Ollerenshaws. Although all differ, all suffer in some degree from depressions. Frances can throw hers off by viewing life as cyclical – and by enjoying food, frequently connected with spiritual healing in Drabble. Her father scarcely communicates, her brother is an alcoholic. The third cousin, Janet, is a compelling case-study of a captive housewife whose misery defines her being. The theory that environment and climate influence our emotional make-up is laughingly expounded by Frances, and developed towards the end in the death from starvation of great-aunt Connie. This assists the plot in bringing all the far-flung members of her family to the funeral; but above all underlines our helplessness when faced with destructive misery.

Drabble considers depressive characters pathological. Janet could not help great-aunt Connie; yet Frances discovers, through old letters in the cottage, that Connie had been attractive once, had had an illegitimate child that died. Implicitly, Drabble contrasts the narrow life of the dead aunt with the potential for renewal in Frances, in the second half of the twentieth-century. 'Yet for some people life is doomed. I tend to have these characters on the periphery. I am deeply sympathetic to the anxieties of the young nephew, Stephen. His suffering is intense, uncontrollable and unacceptable.'[13] Stephen, in fact, commits suicide, but not in an unbalanced state. He argues that 'being alive was sordid, degraded, sickly; tormented by fear and sorrow. Man had been created sick and dying.'

Awareness of the inevitability of suffering affords Drabble a perceptiveness which gives her the confidence to introduce a wider spectrum, a panoramic view of the recession after 1973 in *The Ice Age*. Each character here represents an aspect of England after the energy crisis: property speculation, prison, disablement, capture by Communist power, the gradual running-down of prosperity and enthusiasm. The ability to tackle social issues led to *Middle Ground* (1980). David Lodge calls it 'post-realism', as it uses many of the techniques of realism to capture the fragmentation of contemporary society. Both these later works make conscious attempts to depict society, a role which Iris Murdoch respects, but refuses for herself since she considers art must come first. Drabble's view is that 'one should not try for perfection; it is only essential to feel the work is valid'. *The Ice Age* is

a valid study of the changes after 1973. 'Characters represent
the oil crisis and inflation. What happened to them was what
happened to society. The story is only interesting for what
it reflected of society.'[14]

In *The Ice Age* Drabble develops the social analysis, within
a more complex construction which includes a love-story,
imprisonment and a final clever twist. But the symbols reveal
more than plot: they are what Moers would term 'feminine'
as they represent rounded landscapes, gardening and small
birds.[15]

> I knew half-way through that I needed a bird at the end to resolve that
> particular shape. It begins with a pheasant, a large artificially-preserved
> bird, dying of a heart-attack; this is a symbol of the death of the old
> culture. *The Ice Age* ends with a little rare bird that he sees while in
> prison in the Balkans. It symbolises the human spirit fluttering for ever
> in its rare and special way.[16]

Anthony Keeting in *The Ice Age* is a modern man, an
operator, at one with the spirit of his age. He and his friends
gambled on the stock market, but were no different, in
essence, from the men who built the British Empire. By the
end he is made to realise he is an anachronism, and accept
expiation in prison. He had lived by a patriarchal philosophy
of power which is criticised as destructive games-playing.
This novel ends with a bleak view of one woman's situation
in a man-made world. Unfortunately, the potentially rebellious
woman, Alison, is only half developed. 'Her life is beyond
imagining. It will not be imagined.' Drabble rightly realises
we shall be disappointed. She could be criticised for opting
out of imagining the most pertinent role. She exploits the
role of narrator to excuse her weaknesses. This may prove
endearing to some readers, but leaves others unsatisfied.

Middle Ground is of a more kaleidoscopic structure. There
are echoes of *Mrs Dalloway* in the linking of various characters
in different parts of London in one day. 'Its formlessness',
Drabble says, 'is its message.' She allows herself a slightly
wider range of experiment, trying for a sense of immediacy.
Far more documentary is included than in her earlier novels,
facts as ill-digested as most television news. She included the
documentary element 'almost accidentally', and developed it

because it caught the feel of our cosmopolitan society. 'London is now a microcosm of the world, stressed by the presence of the Lebanese student. We are forced to accept in our houses a high level of awareness of global affairs.'[17]

Middle Ground is not so much a story as a week in the life of a busy feminist journalist, Kate. She has just reached the age of forty; and from this middle ground she surveys her past and that of her friends and family while reflecting on changes in our society. The scope is ambitious: an attempt to encapsulate changes that are taking place now, that we cannot fully comprehend. Brief character studies illuminate different backgrounds, with varying problems, to demonstrate that private life is constantly affected by public affairs. Even in the privacy of our living-rooms we accept advertisers' slogans and scenes of international wars. This assault on our consciousnesses reflects the preoccupation of American and British novelists of the 1970s with global themes.

Although the family is still both supportive and destructive, Kate is also an integral part of a group of friends. Drabble extends the older theme of 'no man is an island'. Kate's friends survive adultery, children's accidents and criticism to reach a flexibility of friendship and a relatively honest acceptance of faults and differences.

Drabble has been compared to George Eliot in depicting a wide range of social groups and their interaction (or lack of it). The aim is to capture the 'inflamed atmosphere' of London at the end of the 1970s, after *The Ice Age*; fear and cynicism about the future have given way to bewilderment. She includes the media, social work, intellectuals, working-class homosexuals, adolescents and two rastafarians – one jealous, one gentle, adding apparent objectivity,[18] through exaggerated enumeration.

A new element is the concentration on the urban environment and its effect on lives visually and emotionally. In previous work imagery drawn from nature had been suggestive of hope. Now hope is drawn from individuals' capacity to survive, to continue to find solace in their own energy and in other people. The countryside has been reduced to a distant farm, bought by a sister, and a passage from Wordsworth quoted at a London dinner-party.

With an American-style enthusiasm to catch the fleeting social present, Drabble concentrates on recent historical changes. She records accurately the loss of union fervour against a background of sporadic strikes; the increasing flow of news and information, changes in fashionable clothes and attitudes. Kate has made a success of her journalism as a feminist and, like many of her generation, is now losing faith in this cause. This dwindling faith in cause is treated with sympathy. Drabble states the dilemma: 'It's a difficult freedom, that balance between personal freedom and the causes one has become involved with in pursuit of that personal freedom.'[19]

Drabble suggests that it is the partial successes and many failures of social change that have led to this loss of enthusiasm. Legislation has given equality to women at work, ostensibly, but the working-class women interviewed by Kate lead lives as restricted by husbands, children, housing and attitudes as their mothers. Funds have been poured into social work, but inadequate mothers and violence flourish: powerfully illustrated in a brief but memorable chapter set in a day-care centre. Drabble treats this with a slight irony that leavens her social analysis, highlighting the discrepancies between ideals and actuality.

Drabble adumbrates other interesting themes in passing, often much too sketchily; she wishes to reflect the contemporary sensation of being bombarded with transient ideas, news items, changes, fashions. It is symptomatic that the heroine works in the media.

Kate makes money by publicising the latest causes: 'Daily newspapers fill us with awe, wonder, sickness and despair'; Roth's observation is caught in Kate's reactions: 'Life is too bizarre for fiction these days.' Faced with this reality, overwhelming for a novelist, Drabble follows television in ranging from one case-history to another: 'but one could go on endlessly, and why not, for there seems little point in allowing space for one set of characters rather than another.' The difficulty of finding a pattern becomes part of her structure. Like Mailer she has included too much, as bizarre reality embarrasses the writer's meagre imagination.

This 'faction' (as Mailer calls his journalistic fiction) is linked by Kate tenuously, by the imagery and by slight irony: 'Kate is slightly ahead of her time, she is responsible for trends and contributes to making them.' There are comic elements in the light-hearted caricatures of *Guardian* journalists, their sense of desperate immediacy and social concern.

Usually, women writers succeed with irony, like Muriel Spark, rather than the broader elements of humour. Drabble includes one farcical scene, a parody of a surrealist play. This introduces another topic: our bewilderment in the face of much modern art. In early novels she had seen culture as humanising, but now the Tate Gallery scarcely helps to make sense of the changing fashions in the 'creations' of Kate's ex-husband, a painter – though she has a moment of revelation in the National Gallery; it is art of another century that comforts Evelyn, the social worker, in hospital. She repeats Emily Dickinson, 'Better an ignis fatuus than no illume at all.' It redeems her own notion of her value: 'Why expect results, progress, success, a better society? All we can do is join the ranks of the caring rather than the uncaring.'

Ambiguity also heightens the study of sibling tensions, usually a strength in Drabble. She uses Russian fairy-stories to stress archetypal love–hate relationships. These stories evoke the closeness Kate experienced to her brother during evacuation bringing in historical reality, and the universality of folk tales, emphasised by Russian formalist critics.

Here the writing becomes more dramatic and imaginative: 'The dirty, tangled roots of childhood twisted back beyond all knowing. Impacted, interwoven, scrubby, interlocked, fibrous, cankerous, tuberous, ancient, matted.' The hectic style attempts to match the fragmentary, but tenuously connected, historical reality. Kate incoherently tries to find sense: 'If you were to roll up your life and mine, it would be something quite different.' Drabble sees that we are part of the historical process, but views this less pessimistically than Kurt Vonnegut and less cynically than Malcolm Bradbury.

CONCLUSION

Her style would be enlivened by some of their experimentation. 'Surely at my age I ought to have the courage to write badly?' she claims defensively.[20] Perhaps, since writing fast has allowed her to capture female reactions with an immediacy that has gained adherents in United States as well as Europe. Her extolling of motherhood bears occasional resemblance to women's magazine fiction, partly because such fiction does reflect female hopes of how the world might be improved in a patriarchal society. Rosamund learns as much from what she calls 'cheap fiction' (i.e. about abortion) as she does from the nineteenth-century novels she admires. Indeed Drabble makes her use clichés occasionally, linking her illuminating remarks and ordinary comments in unpretentious first person narrative with which her wide readership can empathise.[21]

She is conservative in technique, preferring a 'good, traditional tale'. However even male critics such as Bernard Bergonzi have praised the 'genuine newness' of her themes. Her writing in *The Garrick Year* becomes more vivid when Emma leaves her half-hearted lover to plunge into the river to rescue one of her children, showing the supremacy of basic maternal instincts. In women such as Emma she has mirrored contemporary woman's predicaments. The emancipated woman and the mother are no longer two differentiated types, they are combined in the same person, as in her own existence. She might be accused of including too much autobiography. And it could be objected that she admires Bennett's writing too much for the good of her own structures. Nevertheless his type of linear plot has provided useful patterns for analysing women's lives. Drabble demonstrates the flexibility of the traditional novel by adapting it to new themes in open-ended stories, while keeping plot, suspense and character viewed as unified, not fragmented. Her narrating could be called male in that she prefers to be omniscient. At times she is too manipulative: 'In fact Frances was rather pleased that Joy did not wish to become too friendly, as she didn't like Joy much either. So there you are. Invent a more suitable ending if you can' (*The Realms of Gold*, p.356).

In her tenth novel, *The Radiant Way* (1987), Drabble

continues to involve the reader, with sometimes impressive direct interpolations – often leading to 'realistic' anti-climaxes. This new work centres on a trio of relatively successful graduate women. Drabble depicts their friendship as it develops from late adolescence through failing relationships and understandable strains. The strength of female bonding is skilfully represented, in spite of passing jealousies and occasional enviousness. Through three working women Drabble analyses the public and the private, seeing patterns in individual and social experience. In achieving this she considers herself firmly in the tradition of women novelists of the nineteenth-century. She terms herself a 'social historian', ambitiously charting developments from the 1950s to the mid-1980s, with broad sectors of society, from industrial Yorkshire to London, from the working class to upwardly mobile middle-class intellectuals. She approaches the important theme 'What sort of politics should we have today?' In representing the frustrations of women brought up with the hopes of the brave new world of the welfare state, Drabble makes her trio exemplary of the disillusions and questioning of contemporary society.

Like Murdoch and Byatt, she tries to understand male viewpoints, though she is far less interested in them. She is less able, and less willing, to enter a male psyche, though she has the ability to move in and out of feminist perspectives. Her gentle feminism approached some of the issues to be pursued by radical feminists: the divorcing of maternity from sexuality; the effect of maternal instincts on educated women; the use of pragmatic language for female topics. She is percipient about the possibilities of her type of writing:

We do not want to resemble women of the past, but where is our future? This is precisely the question that many novels written by women are trying to answer: some in comic terms, some in tragic, some in speculative. We live in an unchartered world as far as manners and morals are concerned, we are having to make up our own morality as we go. Our subject-matter is enormous, there are whole new patterns to create. The truest advantage of being a woman writer now is that never before have women had so much to say, and so great a hope of speaking to some effect.[6]

BIBLIOGRAPHY

There are two studies of Drabble's novels. Her early works are sensitively examined in *Puritanism and Permissiveness* by Valerie Grosvenor-Myer (Vision, 1974). *The Novels of Margaret Drabble* by Ellen Cronan Rose displays a feminist approach (Macmillan, 1980).

NOTES

1. Interview, 25 January 1985.
2. Betty Friedan, *The Feminine Mystique* (Penguin, 1963), p.9.
3. See Hester Eisenstein, *Contemporary Feminist Thought* (Unwin, 1985).
4. See note 1 above.
5. Marks and de Courtivron (eds), *New French Feminisms* (Harvester Press, 1981), p.260.
6. Reprinted in Wandor (ed.), *On Gender and Writing* (Pandora, 1983), pp.156–9.
7. See note 1 above.
8. Mary Daly, *Beyond God, the Father* (Boston: 1973), p.40.
9. D. Cameron, *Feminism and Linguistic Theory*, (1985) p.144.
10. Toril Moi, *Sexual/Textual Politics* (Methuen, 1985), p.49.
11. See note 1 above.
12. Ibid.
13. Ibid.
14. Ibid.
15. See discussion of 'feminine' metaphors in the Postlude of Ellen Moers, *Literary Women* (Women's Press, 1977).
16. See note 1 above.
17. Ibid.
18. 'It's about the state of London rather than the state of Britain. It's very much a London novel. It's also about feminism slightly and it's about maintaining the middle ground – which is just what Britain is quite good at doing – not being pushed into political or sexist extremism, yet not rejecting new light. I think feminism is a new light and my character is struggling with her feeling both that it is a new light and that it is being betrayed in some fashion. It's more about being female than *The Ice Age* was. It's got no plot; it's very much a texture novel. Because London life is so immediate and rapidly changing I wanted to write about the texture of it.' (J. Todd, *Women Writers Talking*, Holmes and Meier, pp.176–7.)
19. See note 1 above.
20. Ibid.
21. Drabble considers there is not only a female content but a 'female

style. Jane Austen's sentences are so deceptively normal; that is a female style rather than a male style, I would have thought. One could make a fairly good case for Dorothy Richardson and Virginia Woolf being conscious of the female sentence. I think there is such a thing. Not all female writers write in it and not all male writers don't write in it but I think there is a discernible tradition.' (*Women Writers Talking*, op. cit., p.163) This is a contentious area. Many feminists deny that there is a female sentence. See Cameron, op. cit.

CHAPTER 4
Fay Weldon
and The Radicalising of Language

Fay Weldon began writing when women were becoming politicised, a few years after the publication of Margaret Drabble's first novels. Indeed, Weldon's first novels coincided with the advent of the women's liberation movement. She typifies some of the radical feminism of the 1970s in stressing gender difference and its effect on women and their relationships.

Weldon is concerned with relationships today. 'It is women who are writing about the social problems that preoccupy us today, and men are now beginning to follow'.[1] She charts the difficulties not only of marriage and motherhood, but of maintaining any stable relationships. 'I am concerned with the fact that only 20 per cent of women live in nuclear families, that almost all women will have to face the end of life on their own and ill'.[2]

She points out the deleterious effects of one generation on the next with Freudian insight into female masochism – in an attempt to exorcise it. She attacks the domesticising stereotypes which restrict women's potential. Her years in advertising have given her the ability to mock slogan with slogan. 'I was motivated by indignation; there was an enormous amount to be said because life for women was unjust. That feeling started me writing. Women's lives are just as interesting as men's if not more so.'[3]

She shares many attitudes of feminists, though dealing satirically with some of them. The two whose ideas are closest to some of hers are Juliet Mitchell and Germaine Greer. Weldon agrees with Mitchell that four structures must be transformed: production, reproduction, sexuality and socialisation of children. Certainly, Weldon describes more economic hardship than other novelists in this study and occasionally shows women at the workplace – scrubbing floors or typing for dismal wages. Her 'emancipated' mothers are exhausted by the double burden of home and work.

Though she claims the system is at fault, she does not include Mitchell's Marxist underpinning. She raises similar themes to *The Female Eunuch* published in 1970, the same year as *Down Among the Women*: 'Romance has been one of the adventures open to women and now it is over. Marriage is the end of the story' (*The Female Eunuch*, p. 186). They both show how women have been conditioned to hold back, duped by male confidence. They propose revolution should begin in the home as happens at the end of *Female Friends*. The premise that the personal is political is now overt. Greer maintained that women should refuse marriage, a view which liberates a few of Weldon's heroines. They question the opinion that sex is necessary to a full life, though neither is against having children. There is a feminist world view in that they concentate on women's experience. Men are seen as the enemy, however much adored for short periods. The conclusions to Weldon's novels offer hope for change if a female can free 'herself from the desire to fulfill his expectations'.

They both see women's oppression in culture and the mind, while Weldon also analyses the influence of biology. She does not welcome biological determinism. Unlike Shuttle in *The Wise Wound* she considers that childbirth and hormonal changes limit female potential. 'Nature is the enemy of women, giving us painful periods, polyps, headaches'. (*Praxis*, p. 130). Her style is transformed by direct, rueful mention of women's bodily experience. Exasperation and fact are fused with journalese and poetry on the ambivalence women feel towards their bodies. What had been implicit in Drabble has now become explicit.

Weldon produces parables for our time, created out of our every-day existence. This could date her, but I suspect that parables such as *Female Friends* or *Praxis* will last. She is fairly politicised, representing the fighting attitudes of the early 1970s but insists 'now many others are saying these things better than me, so I can be more literary'.[4] She is an acute observer of the changing social attitudes of recent years, creating new myths out of the small worlds of women. 'Things come at you from the newspapers and what you see on TV'.[5] She chronicles change, from the hint of revolt against stereotyping of female bodies in *The Fat Women's Joke*, to the voicing of outrage in *Down Among the Women*, to criticism of world politics in *The President's Child*. Is she too peremptory in interpreting society? She attempts to make sense of our culture by refusing some present-day meanings, thus opening the possibility to different futures.

Among her qualities are the presenting of many points of view, through groups; the conjuring up of a scene, a quarrel, a relationship in a few vivid details; the talent to switch backwards and forwards in time in order to review a whole life with its surprising changes; above all she possesses a distinctive type of humour ranging from mockery to social satire, including the one-liner and farce.

HUMOUR IN WOMEN WRITERS

Until recently women were considered less humorous than men, in spite of Jane Austen's wit, and evidence of female irony since the eighteenth century. Of course, women have been less boisterous and punning, but they had less freedom to mock conventions, make jokes, use daring language or play the fool. 'But at last women are freer as they are not as dependent on men economically.'[6] Now that women can be independent they show equal ability at farce, as proved by Murdoch's *Under the Net*; parody as shown by Rose Macauley, who not only analysed women's status but wittily parodied women novelists: 'unmarred by any spark of cleverness, flash of wit, or morbit taint of philosophy. She bored no one who read her, because she could be relied on to give them what they hoped to find – and of how few of us alas, can this be said!'

Since Ivy Compton-Burnett, women have proved excoriating exponents of black humour. She is even more extreme than Weldon, seeing little hope of escape from social and self-made straitjackets. In the 1960s and 1970s women began manipulating black humour with appealing variety. Muriel Spark led the way with a deft combination of the macabre and the surreal to examine religious questions. Then Beryl Bainbridge surfaced with her bizarre perceptions of the surreal in the everyday, the ironic contradictoriness of events as in *The Bottle Factory Outing* (1974), and many other sardonic, yet hilarious novellas.

Bainbridge, Spark and Weldon take a God-like view of time, disposing of their characters whenever theme or plot demand, to remind us that we cannot avoid death. Their small groups represent human society, threatened by violence and sudden endings and absurdity. They achieve what the experimental novelist B. S. Johnson hoped for: 'that the novel should now be funny, brutalist and short.'

Humour is a technique for questioning basic assumptions, like lateral thinking. By satirising stereotypes, or self-pity, we might escape from them. There is a cutting edge to Weldon, energised by 'anger at the treatment of women. If I had to make a choice, I'd rather be thought of as serious than funny'.[7] At times she seems to be expressing anger for all past suffering generations of women, through archetypal mothers. Two of the mothers in *Female Friends* expected nothing of life and got nothing, wearing themselves out through hard work, and forgiveness, and loving, and keeping up appearances. Her men often resemble stock characters of oral literature, who sometimes resurface in TV comedy: the bully, the lecher, the fussy, the hedonist. We can laugh at them without involvement.

Weldon's humour aims to make us reject ideas and modes of perception 'that nurtured and deformed us'. She is brutal in order to accelerate change. Thus she never bores, while seriously urging women to deny that we are the *other* as first defined by Simone de Beauvoir in *The Second Sex*. She describes farcically the humiliations heaped on us by our hormones, the grotesque situations that childbearing can reduce women to. One of her women has a baby while dying in an air-raid, another unintentionally in her father's bed. 'Humour is descent into bathos, like much that happens to women.'[8] Sardonic humour is illustrated by this sentence: 'Serena, her eyes wide with strain and dismay, did her breathing exercises each day and achieved a lotus position, but little else.' She overturns our expectations: 'Whoring, for male or female, is a way out, not a path down'. Surprise and timing are hallmarks of her language.

Since its beginning in the eighteenth-century the novel has been working at its primary tool – language. Today, in our pluralist society, we have many forms of English: the languages of America, the Commonwealth, the Third World – and now women. Weldon is one of the most accessible and pungent of these new women's voices. Her language is abrasive, with the directness of advertising. She invented the slogan: 'Go to work on an egg.' She has taken the pithiness and spacing demanded by copywriting to lighten her pages. From popular journalism she has adopted the punchy paragraphs, the thumb-nail sketches, the short sentence standing on its own. 'Humour is a kind of punctuation because you can say in one sentence what would otherwise take a page.'[9] From her experience writing TV plays she deduced that plot and brief dialogue must carry the message. She has developed a dramatic style of novel, dealing with essentials only, in media language, easy to relate to. Occasionally she lapses into the sketchiness and crudity of journalism, as she writes fast.

WELDON'S EARLY WORKS

Weldon's first novel, *The Fat Woman's Joke* (1967), is still a valid critique on restrictive images of women. Her heroine escapes because of her husband's attempts to mould her – by making her slim with him. Based on her second television play it is less incisive than later novels, but amusingly highlights the unease women are made to feel with their bodies. Weldon initiates many of the themes she develops devastatingly in later novels and plays: the dissatisfactions of marriage, the destructive effects of consumerism and the misery caused by following traditional roles.

The Canadian feminist Margaret Atwood, in her first novel,

also described the destructive effects on woman of attempting to conform to advertising images, which nullify their heroines, unable to find satisfactory outlets for their personalities. Her *The Edible Woman* appeared in 1969, though she had written it slightly before *The Fat Woman's Joke*. Both writers deconstruct stereotypes of domesticated women with a mixture of realism and irony. They centre on the symbolic cannibalism of women by men. They attack the advertising of food both as a comforter (for the deserving) and a sin (for the overweight). The anorexic heroine of *The Edible Woman* refuses food in an unconcsious rejection of the marriage that would absorb her personality. While overeating for Weldon's heroine represents a revolt against a domineering husband; and against advertising images of women which allow us to see only the young and slim. Susie Orbach in *Fat is a Feminist Issue* (1978) analyses this revolt against societal images which limit women's bodies far more than men's.

Atwood and Weldon were describing anorexia and bulimia before these terms had been invented. With their novelists' attention to what the hitherto marginalised – women – were feeling, they diagnosed a malaise before the male medical hierarchy was able to name it.

This acute social observation has brought them a surprisingly large readership, of men as well as women. *Down Among the Women* has been reprinted many times. Weldon has achieved a great deal for feminism with her hard-hitting humour and punchy brief paragraphs.

'Women's lives contain big themes,'[10] they demonstrate the limits of autonomy, the role of chance, the cruelty of nature, social frustrations and economic hardship. Of course, male lives contain similar themes, but 'they can look after themselves. As a writer I can free myself of the need to be liked, appreciated and not disapproved of by men thanks to being brought up in an all-female environment at home and at convent school.'[11] This new freedom not to placate or empathise with men allows Weldon to concentrate on what women have undergone, and what they can do.

Down Among the Women takes a large cast of women (rather too large) to represent what they undergo and the ironic ways they survive. Through three generations she illustrates three different attitudes to the women's movement: 'it's always existed, but often underground.' Anger at the predicaments of women energises her writing. 'Damn braces,' as Blake claimed. Her very title becomes a refrain, a usefully emphatic technique, more poetically exploited later. Here she begins the poeticising of women's 'gruesome work'. The word 'down' hits us with its multiple associations: fallen, inferior status, kept under, 'we live at floor level' (p. 83), scrubbing. Weldon voices the rebellion against having to tackle other people's dirt. Like Buchi Emecheta in *Second-class Citizen*, she depicts the humiliating low-level work that most women have to descend to, in their own homes – or others'. However the final message is ambiguously bracing: 'We are the last of the women.'

Weldon shares a feminist urge to improve women's attitudes to themselves and their sisters. She recognises that she is in a didactic tradition: 'I want to lead people to consider and explore new ideas.'[12] She resents the devaluation of woman to a brainless sex-object, and the fears and dependencies produced by maternal indoctrination. Her novels show how the powerless can lose their nerve. One message is that women should no longer collude with men, but take responsibility for their own lives, their own choices, their own bodies.

Weldon continues where Drabble led, in frank discussion of gynaecological experience. She has helped women learn about themselves and their bodies by including hitherto unpublishable descriptions of childbirth, menstruation and abortion. 'Doris Lessing showed me the way by first mentioning menstruation. Though I can't relate to her characaters or aspirations, she made me realise I was not as isolated in my female experience as I had seemed.'[13]

Lessing, Drabble and Weldon describe their female experience of biology in order to understand its effect on the mind and thereby gain possible release, for themselves and other women. 'Fancy seeing success in terms of men. How trivial, with the world the state it's in', objects Byzantia (at the end of *Down Among the Women*) – a worthy inheritor of the struggles of Martha Quest. The personal is now overtly political: 'there are other universes to inhabit; once I knew

that, all kinds of reasonable, sensible things became possible'
(p. 231).

Weldon's structure is defter here than in her first novel,
progressing towards a favoured scheme: a group of women
whose lives represent differing sado-masochistic features.
Many women respond as they recognise elements of themselves. And Weldon, like Scarlet, her symbolically named
heroine, 'was an unmarried mother in the 1950's and that
was a salutary experience. I've encountered the frustrations,
the helplessness, the feelings of compromise and desperation
which are in my characters.'[14]

The desperation and frustrations are viewed comically,
concisely and caustically. Her acerbity alienates in order to
enforce reflection. It is alleviated by frequent farcical scenes
as when the couple who opt for subsistence farming are
unable to grow anything.

She is a mistress of irony. The passive wife left destitute
cheers up on being forced to work for the first time. 'Only
the good get punished and I shouldn't think Phil was good,'
remarks a first wife, to cheer a second. In this one sentence
our cultural tradition of tragic justice is caustically rejected.

Girls and older women are shown collectively with a new
voicing of shared female experience. Indeed their comments
often function like a Greek chorus bewailing the fate of
women. The pity embraces the world's prostitutes 'lost to
syphilis, death and drudgery' (p. 200). Like many other
feminists she attacks the stereotype 'whore' showing her as
victim – or even occasionally triumphant (as in two novels
of 1984: Weldon's *Life and Loves of a She-Devil* and Angela
Carter's *Nights at the Circus*). Weldon makes prose poems
with the female chorus, the new sense of solidarity. At times
she creates a momentary 'poésie de la boue' to rid women of
humiliation. It is regrettable that in *The Shrapnel Academy*
(1986) this technique becomes a trifle flippant. 'The moods
and fears of unmarried, childless and no longer young women
are easily disregarded by those in the active, fruitful and
positive mainstream of their lives. I hope, for your sake,
reader, you belong to this latter category' (p. 17).

Weldon foregrounds women's hitherto half-silenced experiences. Her heroines have to be tough *and* soft. This leads to

linguistic difficulties, which Weldon confronts in a challenging, energising style: 'Down among the women. What a place
to be! Yet here we are all by accident of birth, sprouted
breasts and bellies, as cyclical of nature as our timekeeper
the moon' (*Down among the Women*, p. 5).

In this brief first paragraph she has trumpeted the
humiliations of women's bodily experiences. Weldon is no
longer interested in mediating between men and women,
indeed she feels no need to explain or justify the often
appalling behaviour of her male characters. She puts women
at the centre of her novels to find out what restraints and
barriers they suffer. Their novels help to liberate women
from collusion with men's unreasonable demands.

Weldon expounds her aims and methods clearly:

> My desire was to make something new. I'm preoccupied with women's
> state in the world, so I don't run out of things to say. I'm a processor
> of ideas and if I do it with a degree of professional skill, people want
> to know. I had no time to study what a novel ought to be, I just write
> the sort of novels I want to read. I turned to the novel to have more
> control. When you write a T.V. play, it's only a blueprint for the
> director to adapt. My stories have short, sharp paragraphs, like
> advertising copy, because I had a great deal to say and very little time.
> I used to get up at 6 a.m. to write before I went to work. I was unusual
> as I had to work fulltime, on a pittance, while supporting my children.
> So I couldn't begin writing till I was thirty.[15]

FEMALE FRIENDS

Hard-earned economic independence brings a new freedom
for women writers such as Weldon, Bainbridge, Atwood. It
allows them to approach their contentious themes more
decisively – and derisively. There is a release in their ideas
and their language which comes from not having to please
male readers. Weldon points out, 'If my women characters
are more rounded than men this is redressing a balance. I
just make my males behave and talk, I don't add any
justification for their behaviour. Whereas my women are all
explained.'[16]

Female Friends (1975) explains the affection and dislike
which women are able to acknowledge honestly in friendship.

Her three graces were thrown together by chance, by
evacuation in the war. After disastrous relationships a sense
of potential is released at the end, when they decide to live
without men.

In crisp aphorisms, Weldon castigates the masochistic self-
effacement that mothers attempt to pass on to their daughters.
'Understand and forgive' leads her three friends into unhappiness, a lack of fulfilment until they revolt. Not only does
Weldon debunk many social attitudes, she forces us to review
cherished values: 'How foolishly we loved, how murderous
we are' (p. 18).

The 'martyrs' are contrasted with predatory males. The
painter Bates (Beast) who fathered most of their children,
drove his wife to suicide. It is Chloë (goddess of green
crops) who rears them. Her redeeming feature is 'maternal
warmth. . .fertilising the ground, preparing it for more
kindnesses'. *Female Friends* was praised by reviewers for
avoiding tendentiousness in favour of sharply realised character and situation. Weldon gives us both the texture of
everyday life and a universal perspective.

This is a beautifully succinct parable about female friendship, its supportiveness and cruel truthfulness. Through it
she chronicles the amazing metamorphoses of some modern
women. Marjorie, a tearful abandoned child, becomes a brisk,
satirical producer in the BBC. 'Grace, so talented and bold,
now lives off men.' Weldon's technique of enumeration of
the appalling widens this theme: 'The rest of us fear poverty,
deprivation, abandonment and death. Grace fears the lack of
a good hairdresser. She has no doubt been trained to this
end by a series of unpleasant experiences, but she was, I
suspect, a more than willing victim' (p. 15).

'*Female Friends* is also a parable about the self. The three
parts of a woman can hate each other as they know each
other too well,' commented Weldon. Indeed, she often sees
herself as three distinct people. 'A is the overworked mother;
B is the unsmiling, hardworking writer; C is the inactive
depressive. The writing of fiction is, for me, the splitting of
myself into myriad parts.'[17]

She draws on these 'myriad parts' of herself to 'plumb the
well of the collective subconscious', as she states in *Letters to*

Alice on First Reading Jane Austen (1985). There she illustrates her own approach while praising Jane Austen. 'Abstract concepts also nudge for the writer's attention. Truth, Beauty, Love, Justice, Drama' (p. 23). Her inclusion of these universals adds an ironic depth. Love is 'that elation which once so transformed our poor obsessed bodies, our poor possessed minds. It did us no good' (p. 17). The punch-line and the sentiment are poles apart from Murdoch's heroine Gertrude in *Nuns and Soldiers* 'humming with sacred love awareness'.

Weldon's style and subject-matter take her away from the traditional novel which Jane Austen helped to shape. Nevertheless Weldon 'enjoys everything in her' – and shares the moral commitment and delight in irony. She considers that Austen was the first novelist to suggest that the *essence* of the personal and the emotional in fiction is the moral. Weldon prefers them to the psychoanalytical so often prevailing today. As a woman writer she can empathise with Austen's situation. 'She learned to get round the Angel in the House and write while she slept. Virginia Woolf never quite managed it' (p. 22).[18]

PRAXIS

Praxis (1978), Weldon's fifth novel, discusses wider, virtually insoluble social problems through her heroine's eventful life. 'It's slightly bizarre as more things happen than plausibly would to one woman.' Like Figes in *Waking* (1981), she takes a whole life from childhood to dying to communicate the sensations of being a women, with all the limitations of a female body in our society.

> Praxis is a Victorian girl's name; it also means orgasm and for a Marxist it's the moment when theory takes actual practical form. You could say that Praxis' smothering of the mongoloid baby is the turning-point, it's the culmination of everything these women have gone through in our society. Praxis wanted to liberate her step-daughter Mary, who otherwise would be put into a lifetime's servitude by her loving female nature. *Praxis* is a fictionalised working-out of all the meanings of that word, through the trends in our society, which make women victims. I was motivated by the knowledge that there's an enormous amount to

be said about women's lives.[19]

The bare bones of the life are designed to shock: after a fearful quarrel Praxis's father leaves the mother so lonely and distraught that eventually she goes mad, and finishes her longish life in diverse mental asylums. Praxis's first boyfriend prevents her from finishing her degree, so that she shall support him financially and emotionally. She takes to whoring for a time ('it's a way out') and certainly allows her a new start in London. There, dressing 'like a doll' gains her a dull husband, respectability and two dull children. It is only when she leaves suburban marriage that she begins to live, hurting other lives, but not devastatingly, getting another husband and a well-paid job in copy-writing. This enables her to criticise the mores of advertising, its purveying of half-truths and falsifying slogans. When she loses her second husband she finds consolation in the honesty of women's liberation. She gains short-lived esteem editing their newsletter, but then trying to save Mary from a lifetime's servitude to a mongol, loses two years of her life in a woman's prison where 'the stupid guard the intelligent'.

'I went through all the bad words women are called and made her these: whore, adultress, murderess, incestuous, thief, lecher. And she is all these things, but I go through them one by one to explain why these portmanteau words cannot really be applied to women.'[20] Such radicalising of language is recommended by feminist linguists.[21]

Praxis is Everywoman, trying to grasp 'the root of my pain and yours'. Thus the lively action is interspersed with brief Beckett-like interludes written in a lonely, decaying old age. Neither Beckett nor Weldon allows us to forget that we must all face physical dissolution, death and the 'tearing pain of a past which cannot be altered' (p. 12). The poetry of these desolate interludes provides reflection on the action, even occasional wry acceptance of the cruelties of causality. Weldon achieves a wider context to each novel, here questioning if 'we are in the grip of some evolutionary force which hurts us as it works' (p. 13).

Weldon comes to maturity with *Praxis* which was short-listed for the Booker Prize. The message, 'You can't escape your own nature', is viewed both horrificly through marital and mental breakdowns, and constructively, when women unexpectedly take a wise course: the unhappy sex object Irma joins women's lib; the heroine decides to reject bitterness. They finally gain the courage to live their new sense of female importance and cohesiveness.

Weldon exploits authorial intervention to explain her approach. 'It is the battle the writer wages with the real world which provides the energy for invention' (p. 23). Women's reality is seen and quoted from many perspectives: 'We only have till we're 20, after that it's downhill' (p. 126). 'The worm Anxiety plagues maternal life – will it be deformed? speak? steal?' (p. 130).

She epitomises the anti-romantic and feminist backlash against D. H. Lawrence's ecstatic views of sexual relationships in *The Rainbow*. The Lawrentian sexual mystique has been used too frequently to judge the quality of our relationships. 'I could find no books reflecting what I thought, so I decided to write the books I wanted to read; about the fairly gruesome lives of women in this country today. Most women will end on their own, drained of energy, like my mother – or Praxis. At least I rescued her for two more decades. After all, it's a story, not a balanced view of life'.[2]

Nevertheless she achieves a relatively balanced view in this testament. Truth is 'a devil' when it unveils incest and adultery; cruel when the girls discover 'whatever path they took it would narrow and block' (p. 103); finally liberating. "You shouldn't invest so much in individuals", said Irma. "Stick to movements. That's how men get by" (p. 257).[22]

Irma like many of her characters is not 'rounded' as in nineteenth-century tradition, but a type. This technique, learnt from writing for television, reveals aspects of oral literature.[23] In pre-printing culture, types, such as the devil in mystery plays or Brer Rabbit in American stories, meant that the audience knew what to expect. They also rapidly introduce a wide spectrum of *attitudes*: In *Praxis* the innocent weak-willed girl, the embittered lesbian, the sex-crazed vicar, the obsessive TV producer, the sloganmonger trapped in slogans.

A virtual revolution has occurred since Weldon, Carter,

Atwood and their sisters emerged. After her first publications
Weldon said: 'some people would leave the room in disgust
when I entered',[24] whereas now she is sought after to speak
on radio and television.

> 'It's difficult for young women to imagine what it was like for us in
> the fifties, when it was taken for granted that only men could write
> plays and women could never master the technique of television. I was
> lucky, as I was writing T.V. commercials, so I knew that all you had
> to do was write in the directions. Now it's taken for granted that
> woemn can do whatever men can do'.[25]

This has helped her mature from early bitterness 'chaos is
the norm, where men seduce, betray, desert' (*Down Among
the Women*, p. 141) to the acceptance that an ex-husband 'is
as much a victim as you are. He has his image of himself to
maintain as you have yours' (*Praxis*, p. 241).

This maturity is shown in her compassionate treatment of
modern dilemmas such as euthanasia, treatment in mental
hospital and prison, even differing attitudes to the achievements of feminism. She takes on board the destructive effects
of sado-masochism on the self and one's children. She forces
the reader to re-think what women do to themselves and
relatives because of self-denying societal images. Like a
psycho-analyst she wants us to face the truth as 'better than
valium. It's in understanding oneself and one's situation that
progress lies.'[2]

The final pages are speeded up, as she completed them in
two weeks in hospital, waiting for her fourth child, afraid of
possible death from a misplaced placenta. They enunciate
the hope of retrieving something from chaos through the
support and affection of women. The language takes on a
religious simplicity: 'I have thrown away my life and
gained it. The wall which surrounded me is quite broken
down'. Memory gives her a cathartic vision which frees her
from isolation.

PARALLELS WITH IVY COMPTON-BURNETT

With her stringent tone and unusually spare narrative, Weldon seems a voice on her own. But one can perceive a forerunner in Ivy Compton-Burnett who died in 1969. Their brief novels fuse drama, comedy, even melodrama with social commentary. When Ivy, as she was often known, began writing in 1925 with *Pastors and Masters*, her idiosyncratic tragi-comedies seemed to spring from no obvious tradition, and like much women's writing, were marginalised, except by a few admirers.

The similarities between the two are illuminating. Both use the microcosm of the home to comment acidly on male (and female) tyranny. Their women resist marriage when they can afford to do so. Both show how English women interiorise social repressiveness, allowing it to fester. They concentrate on essentials, cutting away details of housing, scenery, even appearance that might distract from the primitive emotions of the id. Life is seen as cruel; behind bourgeois respectability hate thrives, causing frustration, emptiness, adultery, incest, even theft and murder. Ivy Compton-Burnett is more interested in power than sex, though in her last two novels Weldon embarks on 'the benefits and privileges of power, the little tragedies of not having it'.

They are both original in presenting terrible events through plot rather than description. Their dialogue possesses a personal tone, witty, cutting, revealing desires and thoughts that usually remain unspoken. This is illustrated by 'A woman is not fulfilled unless she serves herself'; 'Our righteousness wears out before our bodies'; 'All the emotions of mankind find their place in the family; all the oppressions of class, sex and age'; 'This place where we live is hell and the game is never-ending'; 'Appearances are not held to be a clue to the truth but we have no other'. I have quoted alternately from each to display their brilliant aphoristic ability.

Neither uses many adjectives, places or even faces. They both come over well on radio, as their dramatic dialogues speak to our imaginations about pent-up emotions, loneliness and hatreds. Neither is interested in intense individualising but in the collective unconscious, as their titles declare: *A House and its Head* (1935), *Little Sisters* (1978). Compton-Burnett, who studied Classics, conveys a greater sense of doom, of fate punishing. Weldon, who studied Economics, evinces a distinctive ideology of the 1970s, indicating possible escape. Of course, the artifice of Compton-Burnett differs in focusing on a small group in a claustrophobic setting, with little mention of biology. Weldon, in the late twentieth-century, can foreground the female body, as in *Puffball*.

PUFFBALL

Puffball (1980) is her favourite novel. For the first time women's complex experience of pregnancy becomes the subject of an absorbing fiction. The story line is simple, the pregnancy of Liffey and how she is affected by nature, by her husband's infidelities and by potions from a jealous farmer's wife. 'It's a study of opposites: the town versus the country, science versus magic, cold and heat, fantasy and folklore.'[26]

A puffball is a swelling mushroom which typically resembles a pregnant abdomen; it can also suggest the human brain, and is thus an apt image for the conflict between mind and nature which takes place in the pregnant Liffey (whose name recalls James Joyce's river). Weldon states: 'I wanted to nail down what it feels like to be pregnant. And writing a novel is a similar creative process.'[27] In passages entitled 'Inside Liffey' Weldon gives us scientific descriptions to demonstrate the control over our bodies by biological functions. 'Lunar month by lunar month, since she had reached the menarche, Liffey's pituitary gland had pursued its own cycle; secreting first, for a 14-day stretch, the hormones which would stimulate the growth of follicles in Liffey's ovaries.' She *dignifies* female experience by incorporating scientific language to tell a wide public about the growing foetus and the hormonal effects on a woman's mind. Never before has the struggle between reason and unreason, triggered by pregnancy, been so sympathetically and *dramatically* detailed. Interestingly, the best review came from a man, Bernard Levin, who praised her 'marvellously informative and affirmative work'.[28]

Weldon still gives a Darwinian definition of Nature as 'a chance summation of evolutionary events'. Yet here she effects a reconciliation between subjection to natural processes and acceptance of them. Her sun-goddess Liffey symbolises fertility of body and spirit. She, like her growing child, is 'a life-force, a determination in the individual of the species'. She is admired for feeling herself 'part of nature's process: to subdue the individual to some greater whole.'

Weldon combines scientific vocabulary with emotional reactions to give us a subtle yet detailed view of the power of biology over women's bodies. She describes its purposefulness and wonder while stressing that by our attitudes we control the quality of our lives. We can only help ourselves if we assist nature instead of thwarting its processes.

Here she resembles those cultural feminists who praise the maternal qualities of 'womb-centred' woman. Motherhood rivals sisterhood, self-responsibility and self-determination as her positive standards for women. There are certain features of her work which do not fit into contemporary feminist thought. She might even be accused of being 'unfeminist' in her attitudes to motherhood. Weldon has never followed any particular feminist group as she reserves the right to decide in each novel what matters at that moment in female lives. This is apparent in her comment: 'I don't feel imprisoned by feminism.'[29] Her lack of partisanship is demonstrated in her treatment of witchcraft. Instead of the feminist reappraisal of the lonely old woman curing by her study of herbs, Weldon represents a malevolent, middle-aged mother, attempting to harm with her herbal potions. Yet it is not merely malevolence as 'the doctor and the witchwoman are dealing in the same substances, the dividing line between medicine and magic is only one of degree. When you are pregnant you are much more receptive to a sense of cosmic blessing and cursing, which affects the way you interpret reality at that time.'[30] Through the power of the potions and Liffey's occasional sense of peace with nature we glimpse a cosmic perspective, to become more important in *The President's Child* (1982).

THE PRESIDENT'S CHILD

'There's only people with power and people without power,'
states Margaret Atwood in *Bodily Harm* (1982). This theme
underpins *The President's Child*, published in the same year.
Both feminists now turn to power politics, where murder can
be easy and women's lives dispensable. Atwood's heroine is
a journalist who witnesses horrific murders on an island off
South America. Weldon's heroine works for British television,
bringing up the illegitimate boy she produced after a rapturous
love affair with an American presidential candidate. Both
novels include thriller-type episodes that would make exciting
film sequences, to demonstrate the mercilessness of male
power, still impervious to female values.

Here Weldon gives us Isabel, her most fully realised
heroine so far, a moving portrait of a woman who thinks she
has a sharing, supportive marriage – until her husband leaves
her. Then he tells her: 'The male–female struggle never really
was an issue, Isabel. . . Real power, real influence, is a secret
thing' (p. 210). Frighteningly, we are shown real power
secretly plotting to liquidate Isabel. It is undercover manipu-
lation of power, behind the scenes, of men with money and
guns, that leaves women and children powerless.[31]

The shock tactics of the thriller are relieved by poetic
reflections from a blind neighbour Maia. A modern Tiresias,
she universalises the ideas in striking aphorisms: 'Self-doubt
defines us, as well as aspiration.' She is also used to link
reality and fiction: 'I gather past and present together and
tell them *stories*'. Weldon's story-telling device is used less
crudely here to transmit information concisely, entertainingly.
The blind Maia with her heightened powers of intuition is
Weldon's most succesful chorus, puncturing our illusions
through brief prose poems. 'Misery, distress, nightmare and
cruelty. . .spoil for all eternity. . .the calm face of God'
(p. 219). She undermines, together with the thriller plot, the
liberal hope pronounced at the outset that 'the habits of
culture and kindness are catching – one of the few hopes we
have' (p. 9). Indeed, she mediates eloquently between her
street of ordinary, decent, professional people and the chilling
world of global politics, which we distrust with good reason.

Now that her main character is less schematic, Weldon can imbue her with greater depth of feeling, more contradictions. We are allowed to feel sympathy for her worries over her small, aggressive son, even to empathise with her as she faces suicide. And for the first time there is a paean to physical love. On Concorde's maiden flight Isabel fell in love with the presidential candidate to the White House. They spend two ecstatic weeks together. 'Lovers feel that God, in reuniting them, has made a proper apology' (p. 90). 'He was violence, certainty, power and the promise of everlasting peace' (p. 93). The imagery presents implicit critique of patriarchy that will soon destroy their relationship.

Isabel becomes vulnerable as her affair reveals an unrespectable aspect of the prospective president. 'It's an allegory about power politics, and the way America has treated Europe.' Making a woman protagonist of a thriller allows Weldon and Atwood to criticise the ideology of the genre, and refuse James Bond-type acceptance of the mystique of power.

> Thrillers are sold and read as fantasies, but they are not. This is how the secret service, the mafia, undercover agents behave. I wanted to show how frighteningly easy it is for a person to 'disappear'. I admire thrillers like *The Manchurian Candidate* by Richard Condon (1972), their rules represent a challenge. In fact I tackle different types of writing in turn, and try to master them. In *The President's Child* I decided to use three different types of writing, the thriller, the domestic story and a more flowing style for the blind commentator.[32]

This working at style has widened her resonance and range. Linking private and political preoccupations through a love story is a means to demonstrate the influence of government on ordinary people. This is her most powerful, political and passionate novel.

Politics and the problems of power, once considered male areas, are now being tackled confidently by women. Two of the most successful are Nadine Gordimer's *Guest of Honour* (1970), and Alison Lurie's *The War Between the Tates* (1974). Lurie's acute, elegant study of marital conflict is placed against the background of the war in Vietnam. With compassionate yet acerbic humour she portrays war between two beings who had once been close, war between parents and their revolting adolescents.

Starting with relationships, domestic conflicts and individual aggression (previously considered signs of female limitation) has provided these women with remarkable insight into the springs of violence worldwide, and the struggle for power.

In *The Life and Loves of a She-Devil* (1984) Weldon takes the power struggle back into the domestic arena, but with overtones of science fiction. To get her husband back, a wife steals vast sums to pay for plastic surgery, so that she can be cut into a copy of his small, fair, sexy mistress. Weldon admits:

> This is a slightly frivolous novel, though the first half sets out a feminist position. My anti-heroine burns her house down to cheat him of insurance, gives her horrible children away, then frames her husband to get him imprisoned. She does things which one half of you will applaud, the other not. Next she gets herself turned into a sex object, and lives happily ever after.[33]

Weldon could be accused of perpetuating negative myths about women; however critics such as Margaret Walters praise her for reminding us that rejection can lead to destructive self-hatred. She moves briskly from scene to scene as in the TV plays she writes. This macabre moral parable about the revenge of a scorned woman has echoes of Jacobean melodrama. Its fast-moving brief scenes adapted well to television recently, as they exploit suspense and shock.

THE SHRAPNEL ACADEMY

Hatreds leading to deserved destruction cause the frightening climax to *The Shrapnel Academy* (1986). This gruesome fable on a probable future is sparked by an indignation that has become global. Weldon asks the vital question of why humans allow war. She castigates all of us. 'Now, gentle reader. . . you are as ferocious as anyone else. . . . We all believe ourselves to be well-intentioned, nice, but we can't possibly be, or how would the world have got into the state it's in?'

Her authorial interventions have now become a character, ebullient, chatty, in the tradition of *Tristram Shandy*. She ranges from withering sarcasm to maternal solicitude, apologising for digressions on severed limbs.[34] Her writing can be hectoring and slapdash, yet the intensity of her desire to set the world to rights imparts 'energy, inventiveness and a throwaway expertise in popular mythologies'.[35] She makes us face our increasing destructiveness.[36]

Her theme is war, with herself as truth-teller. Each room in her military academy, named after Shrapnel, inventor of the exploding shell, is dedicated to a general. This allows her to indulge her favoured technique of enumeration of the awful, 58,000 dead here, four million there. Fact is even more terrible than fiction; she should leave it to speak with less authorial intrusion. The characterisation is unconventional and polemical, based on sets of decorative attributes, an anti-humanism which matches her theme. The story reads like a TV script: a group of people are brought to a weekend conference by the country-house device, with a dinner party, hatreds of Upstairs Downstairs and a final filmic explosion.

The views of fellow novelist Anita Brookner are illuminating:

> Weldon is not so cold, nor so destructive as Ivy Compton-Burnett, but this novel suffers in a self-congratulatory diatribe against the inventors of deadly weapons. Where there is too much indignation, the satire vanishes. Her sub-text has always been the futility of men, in comparison with whom women are naturally more interesting if no more admirable. Her name will remain in twentieth-century fiction for an examination of war between the sexes; but the women here fail to make their mark, and the men cannot expand to fill the gap. . .It is perhaps inevitable that a novel on the folly of man should end with an invocation to Nature, a quantity generally held to be female.[37]

This is a timely, provocative satire on the human comedy of errors leading to the escalating arms race.

CONCLUSION

Weldon is a variable writer, too episodic in *Down Among the Women*, too far-fetched in *The Life and Loves of a She-Devil*.

However, her popularity demonstrates that her castigation of our consumer society finds a responsive chord in many. She attempts what she praises in Salman Rushdie 'to survey the lot of millions. There's no point in reading unless you expand your knowledge of life.'[38] Ironically, part of her success stems from providing what many consumers want: easily-digested paragraphs, action-packed stories, a clear-cut message, indeed sometimes too clear-cut. Her experience in copy-writing has given her an original voice, usually energising, but occasionally too obvious. Yet the one-line slogans of advertising transform many comments into moral apothegms (terse pointed sayings embodying a truth).

'A discussion of ethics – that's the only thing that makes a play or book interesting, and indeed justifies the great number of books in the world', declared Weldon in 1982.[39] She is a moralist, often underestimated because she is entertaining. 'A vision of the permanence of love is a definition of innocence.' 'How can we wish ourselves out of existence when our very being depends so much on sin and sorrow?' Such psychological insight and poetic conciseness make her an equal of La Rochefoucauld, praised in the seventeenth-century for his *Maximes*, such as 'We can all bear the misfortunes of other people.'

Her plots have a filmic quality that makes them direct and vivid. Concepts are often presented with visual images, such as a lonely woman writing alone in bed; that is partly why her novels adapt well for television, which she knows as script-writer, adapter and advertiser. Thanks to this Weldon can reach a far wider audience with her modern parables.

Only a short time ago Elizabeth Hardwick thought women writers could not compete on an equal basis with men because of immutable difference in experience: 'Women have much less experience of life. . . brutality, physical torture, unimaginable sordidness.'[40] Weldon (and Toni Morrison and the South African Bessie Head and their sisters) depict women experiencing unimaginable sordidness. Weldon goes further and claims that these hitherto marginalised groups (though enormous numerically) can interpret the state of our society more clearly than males. Inspired by indignation at female suffering, she has produced imaginative parables of women's experience. She has succeeded in reaching a wider audience than many feminists as she does not aim only at a committed group.

She places value on motherhood and sisterhood, but has failed to explore fully her contradictory attitudes to them. Whereas Doris Lessing in *The Summer Before the Dark* (1973) gives a brilliantly empathetic study of a middle-aged woman trying to grapple with these contradictions. Both writers have done a great deal for the self-image of women – and for experimentation in novel-writing. But we should not demand solutions from novelists, Weldon should not be castigated for representing contradictory attitudes.[41]

Weldon is unusually ambitious for a woman writer. Like Anthony Burgess, she has moved from violence in individuals to violence in power-politics. She deals with central dilemmas: how far we can change ourselves, and our relationships; whether we can live on our own, while needing others, to whom our individuality cannot adapt. Indeed one of her aims and leitmotifs is announced by Praxis (p. 14):

> Better for me to look at myself, to search out the truth, and the root of my pain, and yours, and try to determine even now, whether it comes from outside, whether we are born with it, or have it foisted upon us.

Each novel demonstrates her independence of mind and increasing technical virtuosity. Her inventiveness is such that it is impossible to predict her future development. Anita Brookner judges her 'one of the most astute and distinctive women writing fiction today';[42] while David Lodge considers her one of our most experimental and gifted novelists. He asserts that she has achieved 'a conscious and expressive flouting of conventional realism. Combined with a characteristically fluid handling of time, Weldon provides the pleasure and exhilaration of a multilayered narrative packed with surprise, wit, irony and lyricism'.[43] She draws the reader's attention to the texture of language itself, with moments of lyric epiphany punctuating the terse narrative. Her punctuation furthers her aim, with a postmodernist use of double-spacing. In her hands it becomes a poetic device, like pauses between verses.

Weldon may be termed postmodernist in breaking down traditional structures, and even more in pinpointing when the image governs human beings. Barthes maintained (in *The Civilisation of the Image*[44]) that we are in a culture increasingly governed by images which the human subject no longer creates or controls. Weldon with her moral fervour hopes to help us control or at least limit the deleterious effects which cultural and media images of women have on all of us.

NOTES

1. Interview with Frank Delaney, BBC2, 18 January 1985.
2. Talk followed by questions and interview at Morley College, 5 February 1985.
3. Ibid.
4. Ibid.
5. See note 1 above.
6. See note 2 above.
7. Ibid.
8. Ibid.
9. Ibid.
10. Ibid.
11. Ibid.
12. Ibid.
13. Ibid.
14. Ibid.
15. Ibid.
16. Ibid.
17. Interview with M. Wandor, *On Gender and Writing* (Pandora, 1983), p. 166.
18. There are even echoes of the late experiments of the modernist Woolf, in whose diary (21 February 1927) is a fascinating jotting:
    'Why not invent a new kind of play; as for instance: Woman thinks
    . . .

    > He does . . . She sings.
    > Organ plays . . . Night speaks
    > She writes . . . They miss . . . They say

    Away from facts; free; yet concentrated; poetry yet prose; a novel and a play.' Weldon shares the modernists' fractured language and fractured consciousness, their heightening of visual awareness.
19. See note 2 above.
20. Ibid.
21. Such as Deborah Cameron, in *Feminism and Linguistic Theory* (Macmillan, 1985).
22. Reviewers praised *Praxis* for its personal and idiosyncratic view of

women's plight, since Praxis displays exasperating contradictions.
23. See Walter Ong, *Orality and Literacy* (Macmillan, 1982).
24. See note 2 above.
25. Ibid.
26. Ibid.
27. Ibid.
28. Review, *Sunday Times*, 17 February 1980.
29. See note 2 above.
30. Ibid.
31. Both Weldon and Atwood quote from reliable newspapers, incidents such as the shooting of a dictator's ex-mistress and child, to demonstrate similarities between real incidents and thrillers.
32. See note 2 above.
33. Ibid.
34. Deplored by Penelope Mortimer, *Sunday Times*, 6 July 1986.
35. Lorna Sage, *The Observer*, 6 July 1986.
36. Weldon suggests that her characters represent all of us. 'I mean us to face our aggressions. You identify with the characters at first – until you discover what their jobs are' (*Meridian*, 11 July 1986).
37. Anita Brookner, *The Spectator*, 12 July 1986.
38. Review of *Midnight's Children*, Radio 3, June 1986.
39. In interview with Suzanne Lowry, *Sunday Times*, 24 September 1982.
40. E. Hardwick, *Seduction and Betrayal* (Weidenfeld and Nicolson, 1970).
41. Zoë Fairbairns maintains that contradictions spark the writing of a novel and this certainly happened with her feminist novel *Benefits*.
42. See note 37 above.
43. Review in *Sunday Times*, 23 September 1982.
44. Roland Barthes referred to the Civilization of the Image; Louis Althusser and Jacques Lacan to the Ideology of the Imaginary; and Umberto Eco to the Kingdom of the False.

BIBLIOGRAPHY

There is little of academic interest so far published on Fay Weldon, except for one article by Harriet Blodgett, 'Fay Weldon' (University of California, Davis, Cal.), obtainable from Fay Weldon's agent, Goodwin Associates, 19 London Street, London W2.

CHAPTER 5
Eva Figes
and Continental Voices

EVA FIGES AND THE CONTINENTAL INFLUENCE

Eva Figes established her name with the publication of *Patriarchal Attitudes* in 1970. This is a closely argued feminist critique of male attitudes in society, religion and literature. She analyses the ways in which Christianity, capitalism and even psychoanalysis have forced women into subservient positions. It was one of the first epoch-making studies of man-made conventions. She begins with J. S. Mill: 'I deny that anyone knows, or can know, the nature of the two sexes, as long as they have only been seen in their present relation to one another' (p. 10). She ably uses recent research to support her argument that nurture is more important than nature.

In *Patriarchal Attitudes*, women are the starting-point. However, when she began to research, she soon realised she must write about men's attitudes, since they had written most of the books about women. She identifies the principle of male-as-norm, and analyses the way this has limited the development of women. She rebels against the assumption of superior male intelligence by demonstrating weaknesses in male logic: she points out that if men can claim that women are made for childrearing, then women could equally well claim that men are made for insemination. The Judaeo-Christian tradition stressed woman's unworthiness in order to make her a scapegoat. Just as emancipation was emerging, Freud declared that women are passive, suffering from envy! She underlines the fact that men find women dangerous since women can both understand patriarchal attitudes, which they are taught *and* they experience female attitudes.

The book is cogent yet poetic: 'The image in the mirror to which we dance is created by Man; not by men and women jointly for common ends. . .Man's vision of woman is not objective, but an uneasy combination of what he wishes her to be and what he fears her to be' (p. 15). The predominance of man's vision is traced through Bible stories and art to modern education. Even in 1963 the Newsom report, *Half Our Future*, only recommended housecraft for girls not boys – like Rousseau, one of the many male revolutionaries whom Figes attacks for undervaluing half the human race. She supports her arguments well, beginning with a constructive, gender-free definition of the nature of thought. 'We guess, we assume, we construct false theories, moving forward in the only way possible, fumbling in the dark' (p. 19).

Her arguments articulated the feelings of the women's liberation movement of the late 1960s. Her language suggested ways in which these feelings might be canalised into literature. The stereotypes she dissects recur in the images of Angela Carter and Fay Weldon; such as the mirror, the whore, Lilith, or the 'pure' female redeeming sinful male. *Patriarchal Attitudes* is remarkably well researched. 'Yet it took only nine months to write as the ideas had been turning round in my mind, and I found bias everywhere – in Darwin, in Freud, in Marx. I have not changed my ideas fundamentally.'[1] The book includes lively, sometimes amusing vignettes of the education of women since Tudor times, ending with a certain optimism, since she believes that men can benefit from change as much as women.

Figes felt the constraints in man-made language while writing non-fiction. 'Innate male bias in many words is difficult to eradicate; and s/he can be awkward, though often needed. But I feel the constraints far less in fiction, since every writer has to remake language. You've got to find a voice of your own.'[2]

She found a voice of her own through her fiction. Her novelistic style differs from this treatise and her journalism because she concentrates on the inner life.

For style I admire Proust and Woolf most. I tend always to look abroad because I'm not English. [She came here when she was seven and still speaks fluent German.] My outlook is European rather than English, and the writers who influenced me before I began writing were Proust and Kafka. I admire Proust's language, as he includes a whole nexus of considerations. He broke away from the themes that tended to frame male novels, such as power and war. But emotionally I was more affected by Beckett, his despair in the internal monologues.[3]

Her second, highly praised novel, *Winter Journey* (1967), reveals an empathy for the impotence of extreme old age found in Beckett's finest writing. The structure is inspired by Schubert's *Winterreise*; the subject is the conflicting, pointless stream of images in the head of an ignorant old man. His feelings, ramblings and unsatisfied needs are drawn together in a poetry of the inarticulate.

This prose poem adumbrates an unfulfilled lifetime. Like Feinstein's *The Border* (1984) and many novels of Muriel Spark, it is only about a hundred pages. These three women began their writing career as poets. They have brought into the novel the jewel-like compression of poetry, its images, its capacity to express the universal through one individual's emotions. They possess the poet's hard-won ability to create new form for new utterance.

Her fifth novel *Days* (1974) poetically imagines the experience of ageing: 'I write about areas where there's no answer, such as being trapped in an ageing body. My idea was a universal experience which is why she has no name. A name is merely a social phenomenon, not needed when lying half-awake.'[4] A sick woman watches her sparsely furnished hospital room while her thoughts flit from her broken marriage to her present weakness; from her bed-ridden mother to her adolescent daughter. She relives her failures during her monotonous days; the tragedy of the ordinary housewife mother is delicately conveyed, with turbulence beneath the surface. Figes enters a women's mind through interior monologue; nevertheless she eschews the feminine punctuation of Dorothy Richardson,[5] with its unfinished clauses, fragmentation and ellipsis. Figes' sense of form favours the polished sentence to describe 'what goes on in the head'. She claims 'this is what the novel can do best. Reportage is better done on film and TV.'[6]

Nelly's Version (1977) studies an amnesiac 'to expose the inherent ambiguities of a story, as the reader has to question what is happening'.[7] Figes makes Nelly amnesiac in order to show that everything repeats itself. The topic of the novel is the distracted mind, to which she gives us direct access. There is a sense of extreme endurance *and* the mythic questing found in experimental writers in France and England. They link fragments to harness chaos. Figes, Alan Burns, Alan Sheridan (translator of the *nouveau roman*) and Josipovici use penumbra to make sense of the world, of the mind. They exemplify the 'feminine' aspects of the avant-garde artist.

Waking (1981) is her seventh novel, the most satisfying poetically, the one she prefers. She achieves 'verbal imitations of that elusive physiological and psychological process known as thought',[8] which modernists foregrounded, in revolt against the 'factual' novels of Bennett.

The realm of waking, between consciousness and dream, is encapsulated in an original form: seven phases in the life of a woman; seven waking moments in the cycle of her existence, from childhood rising to crescendo with a love affair, descending through middle age to decay and dying. 'I like the idea of form, as structure helps, along with gut intuition. I begin with the shape. I was interested in the relationship to one's body. I wanted something very intimate.'[9]

The intimate relationship of a mind to its own body is subtly caught by shifting from the conscious to the subconscious in the same sentence. 'Yet another February morning, hard as iron. . . I wake back into a world in which everything has become uncontrollable' (p. 61). These impressions are not uncontrollable to us, as she imposes a satisfying overall aesthetic form, easily accessible, unlike the later works of Joyce.

But like Joyce she questions the purpose of the novel and extends it to present an element it can interpret better than any other genre: the mind swinging between rational awareness of waking moments and the irrational world of half-waking. She states that while writing the mind is working on both these levels, the conscious part organising, the subconscious directing ideas and sensations.

Sensation has now become a protagonist. Figes replaces
the desire to know what happens next, that E. M. Forster
considered essential, with the desire to know what feeling
occurs next. Language is now at the forefront, not disguising
its role, but interpreting sensation. 'The *way* you say
something is more important than what you say,'[10] she
maintains.

WOMAN'S BODY AS PROTAGONIST

She extends the metaphor of waking to explore the uncertain
areas between oneself and others, between one state of
consciousness and another, one stage in development and
another. These are areas which men can identify with.
'Women have got to write about experiences we can all
respond to, including men. In the first section I was drawing
on my own childhood memories, to express the magic of
summer then.'[11]

After the joys of childhood, Figes makes us enter the
secretive depressions of puberty, through archetypal images:
'I am running through empty streets. The sky is black. . . .All
my life I have been running. . .now I am exposed. . .I hide
my diary' (p. 27). Gender identity begins to circumscribe her
freedom when adolescent. Once a woman, the body seems
to control her, especially with the shock of pregnancy. 'Lying
on my back, pinned down by the weight in my distended
belly. . . .Night is a choppy, murky ocean. . . .I am tossed
on the muddy foreshore like a stranded whale' (p. 29). Claims
of others crowd her. 'I must move before those contented
sounds become shrill, demanding. . .I live by the hour now'
(p. 39).

The central section is a paean to physical love, recorded
with physical minutiae. Together with the presence of the
other comes the knowledge that it will fade. The infinitesimal
changes while making love give a brief sensation of fulfilment
through the body. Then we are thrown into the heaviness of
middle age. 'Somewhere under the covers lie the remnants
of a body. . . .Life is a river which becomes sluggish as it
reaches the endless sea' (p. 59).

In a perceptive review Sue Roe maintains these are
purely female reactions.[6] Figes hopes that they are not: 'I
concentrated a great deal of experience here and I wanted it
to be universal.'[12]

But as the experience is concentrated in the female body,
she raises interesting speculation about where ideas of gender
identity originate. Figes, like Freud, examines the unconscious
through poetic images, in an attempt to discover where
unconscious concepts of femininity (and masculinity)
develop.[7] To touch on this vital issue she honed a discourse
'respectively tentative, fluid, soaring, then suspended
rhythms; it mirrors the everchanging tenor of the emotions
and apprehensions expressed.'[13]

Figes not only tackles problematic unconscious images, she
uses the novel to 'look imaginatively ahead to solve the
problems that might be coming up in life.'[14] She is never
self-pitying, in the depiction of adolescent rejection or the
elemental state of decay. 'By imagining each stage of life
before I come to it, I overcome fear.'[15] Murdoch also agrees
that the writer dispels fears by analysing them.[16]

This power of words to contain experience is communicated
to the reader through the images that structure the novel.
They are colourful for childhood, black for adolescence, grey
for old age. The sea, to which we all respond, suggests play
to the child, waves of misery in marriage and finally the calm
of death. 'Everything has been washed away in the last tide,
now my body has been swept away I am as light as a bird,
no more trying to find bits of myself' (p. 87).

Figes points out:

> This is not quite stream of consciousness, but an attempt to enter the
> perceptions of a child, later a dying woman. They would not have my
> vocabulary, but they would have these perceptions. I needed this
> stylised narrative technique.[17]

'I chose the female body not for feminist reasons, but
because it's the only one I know. Also the female body, with
its cycle of childbirth gives a satisfactory structure. I needed
the odd number, rising to a climax. It's not based on
Shakespeare's seven ages, but on a woman's life'.[18] For the

first time, the life of a woman's body has become the protagonist of a novel.

Figes has succeeded in an area where Virginia Woolf admitted failure: telling the whole truth about her own body, a woman's body. Figes is one of the few writers in the Woolfian tradition of forging an aesthetic vocabulary for the special nuances of female sensation. She has the advantage of living several generations later *and* not cut off from experiences such as childbirth. Her female aesthetic vocabulary encompasses the reactions of many modern women, and poeticises them.

Woolf forged an aesthetic that championed female consciousness as superior to the public, rationalist, male world. At the time she offered an alternative source of experience and self-esteem to women. Although she overvalued passivity, she imbued fellow writers with new confidence. Many, like Rosamund Lehmann, shared her sense of being a creator acted upon. Figes believes, 'one does not have much choice in what one writes; the topic chooses one'.[19] This reinterpretation of inspiration shows a confidence in the subconscious that 'perhaps women are more able to trust than men'.[20]

She explains, 'I re-read *The Waves* as I had the feeling this was an interesting experiment that didn't quite succeed. The physical thing is missing, which is a form of sensual experience, like language. Hers is too intellectual, but I consciously used it as a model.'[21] Figes goes even further in her attitude to character. 'I take the Aristotelian view that it is by our actions that we are happy or not. It's how people behave in a situation that's important. Character is a myth that can produce caricature.'[22]

This avant-garde view of character shows affinities with the *nouveau roman* and experimentalists like Gabriel Josipovici who seldom name people. They are extending modernism, so that some critics maintain there has been no break. Modernism was an international tendency in arts, especially in painting and fiction (from the end of the nineteenth-century till the 1920s) that pursued impressionism and fragmentation. Aesthetic and formal qualities are stressed, to protect art against the social and historical forces felt to be threatening it. In the novel James Joyce and Virginia Woolf reacted against the social documentation of naturalism by procreating stream of consciousness. This technique attempts to catch the ceaseless, chaotic, multi-levelled flow that characterises mental activity and subjective life. Woolf and Figes combine stream of consciousness with direct comment, so that external life is not neglected, since it has an immediate effect on consciousness.

Modernist writers foreground self-consciousness, in style and/or subject-matter. Like Kafka, they catch modern, fragmented sensibility more acutely than naturalistic narrative.

LIGHT

Eva Figes' novel *Light* (1983) centres on the problem of how to capture the sense of flux, of change in all things. The title is a beautifully apposite image since light accompanies our waking moments, yet constantly modifies our perceptions at different moments of the day. She studies the artist's necessary yet frustrating desire to arrest the passing of time, in the course of one day, which structures this novel.

The central figure is based on the painter Claude Monet. His role is to express any artist's attempt to capture flux. 'It was both his overriding difficulty, and essential to him' (p. 9). The book opens with the patterns of dark and light before dawn, as Claude gets up early to capture the sunrise. His reactions to slowly increasing colour and definition are so clearly caught that the reader is involved in his artist's eye for transient moments. 'The houses lay in the shadow of the hillside, but towards the river. . . green meadows gleamed pollen-gold' (p. 12). The reproduction of 'Water-lilies' on the dust jacket records the sense of tranquillity and transforming light in Monet who inspired Proust to create the visionary painter Elstir.

Figes balances the artist with a representation of Alice, his woman, still in the dark. She cannot forget the unhappiness she has undergone. It forms a leitmotif through the book, to remind us of suffering. Alice provides a necessary dark backcloth to the shifting images of happiness and light. 'She turned in bed, sighing, slightly peevish and resentful, feeling the empty hours stretch ahead, how the walls and dark space seemed to be closing in' (p. 2). Her pain is linked with the death of her daughter, the exploitation of the unmarried Marthe, and Claude's neglect of the other daughter's love. The feminist realisation that women are undervalued by men, in spite of their lifetime servicing, is represented but without stridency. 'She felt vulnerable suddenly, knowing how much her sense of self depended on the little things she constantly did for others' (p. 32).

These reminders of social reality flesh out the texture, as do the thoughts of the servants about their work. Yet their rumbling stomachs and long hours are transmuted through their minds. Little deflects from the central preoccupation with shifting consciousness. She considers, 'Plot is a hindrance, it separates the story and the way you tell it. But it was important to me to have Monet's children, to capture the magic of childhood.'[23] The children are also presented through their consciousness. 'In the shafts of light between window and floor she could see particles moving, dancing and this puzzled her' (p. 13). This child's questioning of the strange effects of light link her with the painter, and the much wider theme of changes in phenomena. 'He touched a petal on the burning bush and thought of the extraordinary theory of atoms and how it was not unlike what he could see light transforming' (p. 85).

THE INFLUENCE OF THE NOUVEAU ROMAN

Light skilfully penetrates beyond appearances in order to examine effects of light, not unlike the 'reality' of atomic physics. In this endeavour Figes was partially influenced by the nouveau roman (or 'new novel') in France. The nouveau roman caught the imagination of novelists in the late 1950s and 1960s. Its exponents shared the conviction that traditional concepts of character and plot were less interesting than theories of fiction. The nouveau roman continues some of the experimentation of the modernists, extending the potential of the stream of consciousness by foregrounding visual perception and new views of 'reality'.

One of the best known here is *Jealousy* by Robbe-Grillet. In this subtle study Robbe-Grillet avoids making direct statements about feeling, but conveys mounting jealousy, menace and passion through careful analysis of changing patterns of sunlight over the floor. Figes depicted rays of sunlight, but to represent joy, expectation, the possibility of creating. These two novelists are similar in representing the intense subjectivity of our interpretation of phenomena.

The *nouveau roman* questioned the invented story, conceived as a fiction, a lie and demoted it in favour of self-consciousness, either in the ordering of events or in the subject-matter. It expressed an urgent critical sense of the limitations and potential of the novel. It bewildered some English readers by eschewing moral judgement in favour of action and above all reaction. The approach is theoretical, but stresses the physical: the eye that observes, the passion that distorts are presented as experienced by a subject who is often nameless. The claim to truth is abandoned, we participate in doubt, in the process of creating.

The *nouveau romancier* (new novelist) involves the reader, like Figes, in an intense world of fragmented emotion and memory. The most powerful is Claude Simon, the Noble prize winner. His *Flanders Road* recreates the bungling and mud of the First World War, interlinked with the anguished speculations of a jealous mind. One of the easiest to read is Michel Butor as he novelises the difficulty of writing fiction by recounting his *Emploi du Temps (Timetable)* in straightforward statements. Preoccupation over the direction of the novel is now part of the subject-matter, enriching the texture.

Figes admires the *nouveau roman*, and particularly its chief female exponent Nathalie Sarraute. Figes explains: 'Sarraute was the best of that group, which made one react intellectually. They performed a cleansing exercise in challenging the whole concept of realism. The avant-garde always clears the ground. The *nouveau roman* helped to open my mind.'[24] Sarraute has an unusual love of English life, our language – and the work of Virginia Woolf. She lived and studied in England and writes excellent English. In a recent article she explained that one of her aims is to convey 'inner movements, hidden under the commonplace harmless appearance of every instance'. She called one of her first novels *Tropisms* as this scientific term describes the shifting sensations foregrounded in the *nouveau roman*. She defines tropisms in a way that exemplifies some aspects of Figes: 'Tropisms are tenuous inner movements which slip by rapidly on the threshold of our consciousness, movements which are *not* as they occur in their original state, as shapeless convolutions and vague agitations but as they appear in my books: precise movements and tiny dramas.'[25] Both these women perceive such dramas as the source of creative energy. They both represent moments of agitation, impressions of sudden terror which illuminate a soul during the flux of thought. Even a novelist as different from Sarraute as Sartre admired this power in her writing. She and Figes make the very difficulty of analysing consciousness into the surface *and* the subject of the sentence; 'The light lost its intensity, his mind its sharp focus' (*Light*, p. 33). Description is now a happening, through the intensity of the image. The image can reconstruct the imagination: 'light spans time, death and eternity' (p. 91). The novel is once again a vehicle for positing metaphysical concepts, but unostentatiously, through images valid to science as well as poetry.

Uncertainties are foregrounded, character deconstructed to patterns reminiscent of music and painting. Most traditional props are dismissed, even the timescale. Mentions of time are used to impose not so much a sense of 'reality' as a sense of aesthetic order. Robbe-Grillet, for example, in *Jealousy* uses a spiral order, to emphasise jealousy.

Figes in *Light* adopts the linear order of one day. Her cluster of images, centred on the effects of sunlight, is as important as the family itself. Claude remarks, 'We live in a luminous cloud of changing light, a sort of envelope. That is what I have to catch' (p. 59). This puts Figes firmly among the modernists since Woolf asserted that life is a luminous halo, a semitransparent envelope of consciousness surrounding us. She added that most writers merely concentrate on the plots, the points of life.

Woolf, Sarraute and Figes take the luminous cloud *and* points of light. They fuse the semiconscious and conscious.

Their novels combine reactions to externals with intense awareness of psychological crises: 'The familiar room belied change, the shift of things. Suddenly it seemed empty, and she was no longer in it' (*Light*, p. 30). They dramatise such shifts of thought, from the familiar to universal subconscious fears. We may be living in a postmodernist age, but the novel, in French and in English, has kept many of the strengths of modernism.

FURTHER EXPERIMENTS

Aspects of the *nouveau roman* still inform modern French novels, especially the writing of Marguerite Duras. Possibly best known here for her film script of *Hiroshima mon amour* (1959), she won the Prix Goncourt for *L'amant* (1984). Like Figes, Duras writes short poetic novels balancing every sentence, every cadence. They both draw on intense, often magical childhood experiences, later transmuted by moments of horror. Duras looks back on the first love affair of a child of fifteen, that took place in the now lost world of the colonies. The girl falls in love with a rich young man to whom she prostitutes herself. They never talk of their feelings, partly because they have no future, mainly because neither guesses what the other really feels. Neither is named; yet their heart-rending love and fears of discovery have a timelessness that proves the strengths of this type of writing.

Such experimentalism is less popular in England, where many novelists are too parochial for Figes. But not Maggie Gee, chosen as one of the Twenty Best Young Novelists of 1983. Her Novel *Dying in Other Words* (1981) centres on the suicide of a young woman writer. 'It begins with a suicide in Oxford and other people's reactions. I'm interested in the idea of a closed story and the fact that others have to make up stories for their protection. It begins like a thriller, but others are fashioning the reality of the girl.'[26] Maggie Gee is experimental in questioning what happens to discourse in the novel: 'I want to write new things, but with stories and recognisable people. It's important to me to be part of a tradition.'[27] She admires Woolf: 'the way she catches life, a kind of female writing that's enormously powerful and enormously precise. If I could get that sense of bright life and colour and sense of flow of things, I'd be very pleased.'[28]

Her most recent novel is *The Burning Book* (1983). 'It's specifically political, as I want people to realise the appallingness of nuclear war.'[29] She typifies the woman novelist today, tackling the most important issues that limit our future – death, senile dementia, the nuclear holocaust, in a 'feminine' style. As Kristéva says, 'Today women writers are using what is traditionally considered 'feminine' (senstations, colours etc.) and a certain sensitivity to language, to its phonetic texture, its logical articulation to express ideological, theoretical and political conflicts of our time.'[30]

CONCLUSION

Patriarchal Attitudes was published in 1970, the year when the recent women's movement reached a political dimension, influencing more women than ever before. In this book Figes recovers women's historical experiences, as she recovers their bodily experiences in *Waking*. She is in the Anglo-American tradition in her polemical writing, highlighting the areas where women had been unrepresented, even silenced. She displays affinities with French feminists in using bodily language, previously muted, to subvert existing systems which had suppressed female difference. Thus language can be a revolutionary force, opening the way to new possibilities. It is not so much her sentence-structure which is 'feminine' as her focus. Until recently women had been denied 'full' subjectivity; Figes makes subjectivity central, valuable in itself.

Figes is more influenced by European writers than the other women novelists in this study. She experiments with form, areas of mind and language in ways that are far more European than American. She shows that art reacts as much to art as it does to society. The Russian formalists first pointed out patterns in literary movements, definitely apparent in the English novel since the war. The reaction against experiment in the 1950s rejected Joyce and Woolf. The avant garde of the 1960s and 1970s rejected this rejection, declaring the traditional novel exhausted.

Josipovici, author of *The World and the Book* (1960), maintained that 'experimental writers reveal the potential in each moment, each word, each event, a potential denied by the linear way we live our lives and read our books.' Using the potential of each word to reveal the potential in each moment is something Figes shares with Woolf. They both feel their way towards Woolf's hopes of an 'amalgamation of dream and reality, that perpetual marriage of granite and rainbow'. They impose modernist order on contradictory experience, unity on chaotic flow. Their experiments achieve moments of wholeness in a disintegrating world.

These are central to *Waking*, together with the premise that the body can be a source of self-knowledge. Figes is contemporary in representing the changes in one woman's sexuality over time, changes which stress diversity. In rejecting the traditional concept of character, Figes approaches Kristéva's demand for a radical deconstruction of the subject. Both posit language as a complex process rather than a monolithic system, and wish to deconstruct barriers between linguistics, rhetoric and poetics – though for differing reasons and in differing ways. Figes is a shrewd literary critic also and in *Sex and Subterfuge* (1982) examines the strategies open to women novelists in the eighteenth-century to represent their experience of social constraints. Her recent novel *Light* represents both *jouissance* and a skilful contemporary modernism. She highlights the aesthetic and implicitly revolutionary element in women's writing in sensitive experimental discourse. Her recent novel, *The Seven Ages* (1986) combines folklore and imagination in a powerful novel dealing with centuries of history from women's point of view.

NOTES

1. Interview, 4 May 1983.
2. Interview, 21 August 1984.
3. See note 1 above.
4. Ibid.
5. The question of whether there is a feminine sentence has been

problematised. Drabble thinks there can be; Toril Moi (among others) disagrees – see her *Sexual/Textual Politics* (Methuen, 1985), and *Writing and Sexual Difference*, ed. E. Abel (The Harvester Press, 1970).

6. In 'To plot or not to plot', Radio 3, 14 January 1984.
7. Ibid.
8. From Northrop Frye, quoted by C. Belsey, *Critical Practice* (Methuen, 1980), p. 25.
9. See note 1 above.
10. Ibid.
11. Ibid.
12. Ibid.
13. Sue Roe, *The Literary Review* (1981), p. 13.
14. See note 1 above.
15. See note 2 above.
16. Maggie Gee also states words give power in a world where women often feel weak.
17. See note 1 above.
18. Ibid.
19. Ibid.
20. Ibid.
21. Ibid.
22. Ibid.
23. Ibid.
24. See note 2 above.
25. *Romance Studies*, no. 4, p. 2.
26. 'A Room of One's Own', Radio 4, 10 June 1984.
27. Ibid.
28. Ibid.
29. Ibid.
30. *New French Feminisms* (Harvester Press, 1981), p. 165.

CHAPTER 6
Anita Brookner
and The Woman's Novel

Women mothered the novel, according to Dale Spender and Marilyn Butler.[1] Male critics taught us it was fathered by Defoe (*Robinson Crusoe*) and Richardson (*Clarissa*). But women had begun, long before them, developing a novel form. The first we know is *The Tale of Genji* written by Lady Murasaki in eleventh-century Japan. It is the world's first psychological novel, of phenomenal verve and originality. Genji is the great lover, irresistible, talented, sympathetic, a prototype. *The Tale* is not only a romance, a fantasy about a better, earlier world, but realistic, forthright and unsentimental.

In seventeenth-century France women wrote many novels about how to love (*la carte du tendre*). The most absorbing is by the aristocratic Madame de la Fayette. *La Princesse de Clèves* (1678) is a beautiful study of an unconsummated love affair, ending with acute psychological insights into the reasons why the intelligent, perceptive heroine finally decides not to marry the aristocrat she passionately loves. Madame de la Fayette offers both daydream, erotic longing for the 'prince' *and* a rewriting, in the knowledge that things will not end happily ever after.[2]

When women started writing in England we find similar combinations of age-old romance together with psychological realism. The hundred women novelists before Jane Austen[3] came from the emerging middle class. It educated its daughters, but not in the Latin and Greek of their brothers. Deprived of the privilege of a classical education, girls listened more carefully to contemporaries talking. Their language was thus less rhetorical, with freer structures, more attuned to conversational rhythms.[4] The novel was one of the few forms that had not been appropriated by men. Women were allowed to use it, to fuel it with their preoccupations. The novel became a feminised form in which marriage, the crucial event in a woman's life, was seen as central. Female narrative was usually lively and straightforward. Some plots include adventures, rapes and raptures, like those of Eliza Heywood. Others make bold social comments, like Mrs Inchbald, an actress, so much more emancipated than most of her sisters. In her, as with Aphra Behn, we see the liberating effect of the theatre on the novel.[5]

NEW WAYS OF READING WOMEN'S NOVELS

Revisionary ways of re-reading women's novels have been posited recently. They may be read to uncover biases or omissions in dominant male literature, or to examine how far female identity is not what it is assumed to be. We can decode the sentimental writers if we realise they are expressing a specifically female response to patriarchal culture which undervalues love. Bestselling authors such as Georgette Heyer and Catherine Cookson can be viewed as surrendering their inner freedom into rapturous conformity in order to gain worldly success and divine grace. Their romances are the type written by the heroine of *Hotel du Lac*, who 'believes every word she writes'.

Anita Brookner's novels have worthy forebears in the many women novelists of the eighteenth-century now being revalued by feminists. Eliza Heywood, Charlotte Lennox, Maria Edgeworth and one hundred others[6] were underestimated by male critics such as Leavis because they could not analyse the world of work from which they were excluded. Many adapted romance, the medieval story of hero or heroine in quest of adventure or virtue, setting it within the psychological realism of a woman's emotions. Thus they combined the fictional allegiance to an ideal world with an empirical observation of female reactions. Eliza Heywood has an almost post-Freudian understanding of sexuality, while Fanny

Burney wrote of the material traps in marriage. Women took
the courtly conventions of male wooing and revealed men to
be more calculating and money-minded than they had
admitted. Brookner's males are in this tradition. The
reasonable Neville comments: 'Without a huge emotional
investment, one can do whatever one pleases' (*Hotel du Lac*,
p. 94).

By the end of the eighteenth-century women were writing
with skill and authority, gaining confidence and experience
from each other. They made aspects of the medium their
own: romance and the domestic setting. They developed two
basic plots that have not varied greatly; partly because they
are archetypal stories, partly because they are based on female
experience: There is the tragic plot of seduction and betrayal,
nowadays replaced by falling into bed followed by rejection.
There is the comic plot of courtship and marriage, elaborated
with farce and black humour recently.

The peculiar shape of a heroine's destiny in novels by
women, the sometimes improbable twists of a plot in these
stories should be read ideologically. A happy ending is a
refusal of seduction, of the reifying of woman. The pious
heroine who achieves marriage is asserting her strength against
those who consider her an empty vessel. The sentimental
cult of domesticity represents pragmatic feminism establishing
a place for women. Whereas the tragic ending, equally
common, as in Brookner, represents woman as prey, or
marginalised in a society which accords no value to woman's
angle of vision.

The images presented are usually of women defining
themselves in relation to a man. Those without men are
seldom considered liberated, but rather haunted by loneliness,
like Brookner's protagonists.

In *Hotel du Lac* Brookner explains her approach through
the heroine, an author of romantic fiction. She justifies it
because

> women prefer the old myths. . . .They want to believe they are going
> to be discovered, looking their best. . .by a man who has battled across
> continents abandoning whatever he may have in his in-tray, to reclaim
> them. Ah! If only it were true.' (p. 27)

ROMANCE

Romance depends on the acceptance of a code, such as courtly love in the Arthurian legends or the 'sublime' in Mrs Radcliffe's *The Mysteries of Udolpho*. It is instructive, sometimes moral in showing us an ideal, as in the popular eponymous medieval *Roman de la Rose*. In twentieth-century women novelists this has become the ideal behaviour of men in love. Brookner adopts the romance's simplifying of character, with a few clear idiosyncrasies to set people apart. Romance deals with longed-for fulfilment of desires, often in passionate love, and can end tragically or happily. It is insightful in revealing the forms of an age's sensibility, the longings which cannot otherwise find expression. Its territory is the unconscious mind; it uses fiction to remake the world in the image of desire. It flourishes in periods of rapid change, such as twelfth-century France, Tudor England, the early nineteenth-century and today.[7]

Such allegorical romance must be distinguished from twentieth-century popular romantic novelettes, of the type written by the heroine of *Hotel du Lac*. An astounding fact is that these are so popular that in 1983 alone 250 million women throughout the world bought a Mills and Boon romance. Of course, lovers in fiction have met, separated and been blissfully reunited since Alexandrian Greece, but only recently has romance been aimed so exclusively at women. Indeed, market research promotes it and ensures that cheap paperbacks are available in supermarkets. Its plot centres on a virgin who meets a masterful, successful, older male and is alternately pursued and rejected by him until he finally offers marriage. Why is such pulp-fiction so widely read? It could be argued that this is the female equivalent of soft porn, and superior to that, since more is left to the imagination. And concentration on courtship focuses on the crucial moment when a woman's survival skills are put to the test, and she enjoys fleeting power. There is occasional critique of male supremacy in office and bedroom, but the endings show women still as wholly satisfied to devote their lives to one man – as Brookner heroines discover to their desolation, since they do not meet the masterful man purveyed by books: 'Mimi knows instinctively that she was meant to be the wife of a man so inevitably, so truly loved that he would validate her entire existence' (*Family and Friends*, p. 132). But the man runs away with her sister. . .

FEMINIST LITERARY CRITICISM AND THE WOMAN'S NOVEL

Feminist literary criticism enables us to see greater complexity and social critique by looking at the implicit ideology of women's novels, which are not necessarily feminist. This is a problematic issue; for the sake of brevity I suggest a 'woman-centred' novel may or may not be implicitly feminist but can be read by feminists for its critique of social institutions, whereas a feminist novel foregrounds consciousness-raising.[8]

Until recently there has been a contradiction between ideological and appreciative approaches to literary criticism. Sartre and the Marxist Macherey both experienced this dilemma. They claim the literary work is inextricably linked to the life that produced it, yet it is none the less autonomous in being defined and structured by laws unique to its form. However a late 1980s analysis, using both autobiography and politics like the Anglo-American feminist literary critics, and combining a French linguistic approach can overcome contradictions.

Contemporary criticism gives us the possibility of seeing the old world from new perspectives. A woman-centred approach highlights the female imagination for the first time. Spacks, in *The Female Imagination* (1975), defines a feminine aesthetic transcending politics. Jehlen maintains that because the fictional world is subjective it is ideological.[9] If ideology signifies a subconscious outlook, then both attitudes can be combined as we analyse how a novel transforms ideology into myth, life into literature.

Since its inception the basic structure of a novel has frequently been an impotent feminine sensibility; this represents ways in which the novel implicitly criticises the structures of society. When women place themselves at the centre they are writing in search of wholeness, finding action in spite of dependence. Writing becomes a conceptual and linguistic act of creation of self. We see 'the painful contradiction of women becoming powerful not by overcoming but by exploiting their impotence'.[10] Brookner agrees: 'I write out of a terrible feeling of powerlessness.'[11]

THE WOMAN'S NOVEL IN THE TWENTIETH CENTURY

There is a wealth of women novelists in the twentieth century who have only recently been revalued, from Edith Wharton, Kate Chopin and Willa Cather (in America) to Rose Macauley, Jean Rhys, Rosamund Lehmann, Elizabeth Bowen, Barbara Pym and Elizabeth Taylor. They have inherited many of the qualities of Jane Austen: superb structuring, delicacy, restraint, common sense and devastating social judgements. Women's publishing houses have restored valid women's traditions.

Brookner shares with these writers (particularly Edith Wharton and Elizabeth Bowen) the ability to represent the social frustrations and intimate thought-processes of gifted, undervalued women. They understand the suffering of women morally alone, the vulnerability of the ingenuously affectionate in a scheming, conventional society. 'Innocence so constantly finds itself in a false position that inwardly innocent people learn to be disingenuous, to exist alone.'[12]

Brookner displays, like Bowen and Lehmann, what might be termed a 'feminine' sensibility in the subtle descriptions of appearance, textures, social nuances. They are gifted at linking character and background, representing the restrictive effects of environment on a girl's psyche. They possess the power to render the external world so that it becomes itself a character, rather than a setting.

These women writers invest a special symbolism in houses. Houses both limit and protect women, who can transform walls into a world. Eva Figes argues that this reveals an aspect of the 'female imagination'.[13] The very titles *Mansfield Park*, *Wuthering Heights* and *Hotel du Lac* demonstrate how women turn a restrictive building into a potent social, moral, even emotional image. This is exemplified by Bowen's *The Death of the Heart* (Penguin, 1962). Here the wealthy repressive London house represents an implicit attack, worthy of Jane Austen (or a Marxist) on the corrupting effect of possessions. It is contrasted with the rickety, exciting, impermanent seaside guesthouse, which symbolises loss of innocence, a blunting of integrity, a blunting of the ability to love. The image of the house, with elements of sanctuary and prison, represents the continuing cultural restrictions felt by women.

The well-crafted women's novel has continued to flourish in Britain more than in America or France. It has now attracted the public praise of male critics. Larkin highlights Pym's 'unique ear and eye for the small poignancies and comedies of everyday life'.[14] Their heroines poignantly ask, and get too little from life. Anne Schlee (author of the delicately powerful *Rhine Journey*[15]) pinpointed one cause of this: 'The Victorians have influenced us most. They were real for me as a child, not set in the past. They have an underlying role in my stories.'[16]

It was the established Lord David Cecil who rehabilitated Barbara Pym after a decade of neglect: 'Her unpretentious, subtle accomplished novels are for me the finest examples of high comedy to have appeared in England during the past 75 years.'[17] Pym, and Brookner at times, explore the comic potential of the 'felt' novel while others such as Jean Rhys exploit its tragic potential. Pym ends on a wry, amused note, while Rhys's heroines are doomed from the start – and Brookner's end unhappily. These women writers adapt their lived experience of romance to examine female reactions to falling in love, within a still circumscribing society.

INFLUENCE OF THE EIGHTEENTH AND NINETEENTH CENTURIES IN BROOKNER

From eighteenth-century women's novels Brookner has taken a polishing of form, excluding extraneous themes. She believes, 'It's form that's going to save us'.[18] Like her forebears in both the eighteenth and nineteenth centuries, she shows us what it *feels* like to be a certain kind of isolated woman. Like many of their heroines, a Brookner protagonist turns exasperation against herself in the form of self-annoyance, unhappiness, even illness. Brookner can therefore be studied in the way Showalter and similar feminist critics study nineteenth-century women's literature. They see it as mirroring life, as conveying the suppressed frustrations of the author. Certainly, Brookner admits that she uses her own loneliness, her own family. 'Mine's a dreary Victorian story; I nursed my parents till they died.'[19]

She sees a Victorian inheritance as creating the dilemmas of her protagonists. They are imbued with nineteenth-century values of seriousness, self-control, rectitude – but living in the twentieth-century, which no longer values them. However, Brookner still admires them, particularly as epitomised by the novels of Trollope, with his clear moral judgements. His heroines feared the consequences of indulging sexuality, which has been diminished today by contraception. But the fear of being rejected remains strong, conveyed by Brookner's brief, clipped forms, and occasional repressed phrases.

Brookner's images represent women limiting the notion of themselves from within. Our images create the world for us; they shape our consciousness. The English novel since the eighteenth century has shown images of women in a private domestic world. Brookner continues this association between women and private feeling. She explores eighteenth, and nineteenth-century concepts of femininity and finds many of them still valid. She leaves the reader to ponder how far they are inculcated by upbringing (nurture), how much by heredity (nature).

BROOKNER AND THE TWENTIETH CENTURY

Brookner wryly asserts, 'I write out of a sense of injustice. In some curious way only fiction-writers are telling the truth.'[20] There is a twentieth-century awareness of contradictions in Brookner's double vision of the function of fiction. Like feminists, she realises the damage it can inflict by purveying limited views of women, emphasising cultural conditioning. Yet her heroines are lecturers or art historians, interpreting and moulding their material into presentable forms. The very act of writing offers possibilities for shaping one's life, reworking incidents, giving them a more satisfying form. 'Novels are the chance to examine within the limits of a structure.'[21]

The twentieth-century structures she most admires are those of Rosamund Lehmann and Elizabeth Taylor. They continue the tradition of the lonely heroine not getting what she wants since she is doomed to fall for a man incapable of satisfying her. Brookner is particularly skilful at empathising with the wishes and hopes of the lonely, those who feel they are 'drifting and obscure'. They fear to thrust themselves forward in case they are rejected; they are too repressed to seduce or allow themselves to be seduced. This is movingly represented in two harrowing pages on Mimi in *Family and Friends* (1985). She has gone to Paris to bring her sister home and finds the man they both want. For one lonely disturbing evening she waits for him in her hotel while he is being seduced by her sister. She goes through all the emotions of a love affair, the longing, the responsiveness, the abandon, on her own. All her vitality is suppressed, her failure to seduce leaves her incapable of responding for the rest of her existence. 'The intense darkness envelops her, envelops also her inviolate dream. At some time in that interminable night she lies down on her bed; on her face the smile is tinged with intimations of the most absolute horror' (p. 71).

Brookner acknowledges through some of her characters that there are other ways of coping, such as living for oneself or rejecting the idea of a harmonious love relationship. She respects these attitudes, yet cannot adopt them *emotionally*. In this she symbolises twentieth-century tragedy, a rational capacity to understand undermined by an emotional incapacity to adapt. In ways she is a unique phenomenon because she writes such well-crafted serious women's novels which are also bestsellers. Her popularity gives insight into one aspect of women's writing today, and into what some women readers identify with.

ANITA BROOKNER'S SIX NOVELLAS

Brookner's six skilfully crafted brief novels survey aspects of femininity and romance today. Her first, *A Start in Life* (1981), brilliantly restructures elements of autobiography, centring on the unhappy life of Ruth, repressed by selfish parents. The opening sentence throws us into a central preoccupation, wittily and succinctly: 'Dr Weiss, at forty, knew that her life had been ruined by literature.' The literature is the nineteenth-century novel, particularly Balzac's *Eugénie Grandet*. Eugenie loved in vain, too unpretentious and unattractive to win the man she adored. Such books have imbued Brookner's protagonist with role-models that make her incapable of adapting to the changed ethos of the twentieth-century.

Brookner's second novel, *Providence* (1982), examines the suffering of etiolation such inadaptation causes the individual woman. There is little overt experimentation with language or form, though a mastery of subtle expression and structuring. *Look at Me* (1983) begins and ends with notions of the circularity of time and memory. It is a scrupulous, passionate study of an unsuccessful, obscure protagonist – which is how she sees herself. Like *Jane Eyre* Brookner's heroines long for intellectual and emotional fulfilment through one man, while fearing frank sexuality. The novels are 140 years apart, yet exhibit a similar tension between longing and restraint, instinct and reason. Brookner, like Rebecca West, represents similar protagonists condemned to loneliness because their upbringing has repressed spontaneity, culture has cramped instinct.

Brookner's fourth novel *Hotel du Lac* (1985) won her the Booker prize and established her reputation. It concentrates on a writer of romantic novels, Edith Hope, banished temporarily to Lake Geneva. She had, in wry self-protection, told her taxidriver to drive away when she sighted her uninspiring fiancé on the registry steps. 'Then she saw, in a flash, but for all time, the totality of his mouse-like seemliness' (p. 129).

Hotel du Lac was awarded the Booker prize as a 'work of perfect artifice'. In interview at the time she admitted:

When I started I simply wanted to write a love story, in which something unexpected happened and love triumphed. Of course the image of the still, grey waiting hotel where I stayed remained in my mind. It's a personal story and I meant every word. I know intimately what it's like to be lonely, perceptive, an observer.[22]

The protagonist's life and thoughts bear a painfully close resemblance to Brookner's. 'There were five novels, to prove she had not spent her time gazing out of the window like the Lady of Shalott. It was, she recognised, a tortoise existence, despite the industry. That is why she wrote for tortoises, like herself' (p. 30).

Edith Hope realises she will not be read by the hares who win races, nor the 'multi-orgasmic' girls who get careers and lovers. She is romantic in glimpsing the possibility of passion, yet views it sadly as almost unattainable for the sensitive woman. As for Jean Rhys and Rosamund Lehmann, for Brookner love focuses a woman's whole existence. Indeed, Edith confides to her agent, 'you thought I wrote with that mixture of cynical detachment and satire that is thought to become a modern writer in this field. You were wrong – I believed every word I wrote' (p. 181). Brookner incarnates the Platonic longing for the other matching half. She does not deride novelists like Barbara Cartland who make millions peddling 'a belief in beauty which we all need'. Indeed, Brookner takes formal risks in her proximity to romantic novelettes, but skilfully distances their sentimentality with devices such as flashbacks, irony, imagery and occasional withholding of information. There is a series of letters to a lover and only at the end does she admit, 'This is the last letter I shall ever write to you and the first I shall ever post.'

Hotel du Lac is skilfully constructed, chapters end in mild suspense and only slowly do we discover the truth about fellow guests, as in Bowen's The Hotel. Mrs Pusey, the archetype of the grasping sensual woman, who 'makes a cult of herself' (p. 146), though elegantly painted, is 79; while her apparently devoted daughter Jennifer sleeps around. Ironically, Brookner makes her heroine novelise the hotel guests, but they keep developing surprising dimensions. Every person Edith meets she gets wrong initially. The creating of this fiction is a process of discovery about what these other women are like, above all about what she is like.

Brookner quietly dramatises the emotional void of both the greedy, sexy women and the quiet rejected women. 'No one considered our hopes and wishes. Yet our hopes and wishes are what should be proclaimed most strenuously if anyone is to fulfill them.' (p. 150) Their unfulfilled hopes, their atrophied spontaneity are symbolised by the 'vast grey lake, spreading like an anaesthetic towards the further invisible shore' (p. 1). Fortunately this compelling imagery of a 'climate devoid of illusions' is relieved by a sombre wit. 'The inhabitants are frequently rendered taciturn by the dense cloud for days at a time' (p. 7).

The discreet hotel sanctuary is penetrated by two males; one through memory and wish-fulfillment only. Edith writes letters to a lover, an artful eighteenth-century device which catches the speaking voice and communicates sexual longing. She longs for a passion which ends in domesticity: 'all I crave is the simplicity of routine, an evening walk, a game of cards' (p. 98). An impossible wish for Brookner's heroines. The other man is a rich manufacturer, Mr Neville, a widower. He represents a Jane Austen type of rationality as he proposes marriage. 'Without self-love you will never learn the rules, or you are going to learn them too late and become bitter. You are a lady, they are rather out of fashion. But as my wife you will do very well. Unmarried, you'd look a bit of a fool.' (p. 165). 'Modesty and merit are poor cards to hold' (p. 166). He offers the chance of marriage based on common sense and respect. But when she glimpses him emerging from Jennifer's bedroom, Edith decides to return to her little London house, because 'I should lose the only life I ever wanted though it was never mine to call my own' (p. 184).

This sad yet dignified ending underlines a sense of inner homelessness. Edith voices the lot of all those who feel they cannot accept their lot, yet attempt to do so with the outworn precepts of a lost faith (incompatibility) and an irrelevant moral code. She represents 'the almost successful tenor of an artificial and meaningless life which had been decreed for her own good by others who have no real understanding of what her good was' (p. 116). Brookner writes about the gap between what people feel they are and what they wish to be;

'this is the story of many of us and it reminded me astonishingly, of the great characters in Proust'.[23]

Brookner surveys women today and finds them all wanting. The central characters, like Edith, inherit Victorian ideals of suitable behaviour, buoyed up briefly in adolescence by hope (which is her surname). Through them Brookner investigates the possibility of women living alone with dignity, but like Charlotte Brontë, decides this is well-nigh impossible, as society will deride them. They feel they will never learn the 'rules of the game' which let the lucky few get men and money. Brookner is explicitly naive in maintaining there are 'rules of the game'; but implicitly realises that the rich few who use their attractions to consume men only *seem* to get what they want. Mrs Pusey betrays a fear of death 'which she must distance until her momentary weakness is seen as someone else's fault. That way the shadow of her mortality will be exorcised' (p. 143). Yet Brookner admires her as the 'embodiment of the kind of propaganda no contemporary woman could stoop to countenance for Mrs Pusey was not only an enchantress in her own right, she was also appreciative of such propensities in others' (p. 39). Edith asks herself what behaviour most becomes a woman, 'a question she had failed to answer and now saw of utmost importance' (p. 40). However, she finds only women who share their sadness, while 'Their joy they show off' (p. 149). They have so few interests, so few ways of judging their value that they represent leitmotivs of unhappiness rather than becoming behaviour, or role-models that might help the protagonist.

The imagery of *Hotel du Lac* symbolises alienation. There is silence on the alienation suffered by men and by working-class women, because Brookner concentrates on the alienation of her central figure. The distant misty autumn lake represents the perfect background to her story, in the English tradition of mirroring the moods of the protagonist in nature.

Brookner's sensitive discourse for place and mood represents restricted lives. The almost unhappy endings provide a critique of the moral attitudes which circumscribe women. 'How like a lingering illness sentiment can be,' the matriarch remarks in *Family and Friends* of her rejected daughter (p. 182).

Brookner's vision is disturbingly paradoxical. Contemporary society allows some intelligent women to enter hitherto male professions, such as lecturing, with their attendant demands. On the other hand, our society still places too high a value on romantic love. Even when her grasping, sexy women get their men, they are not happy because reality breaks in, in the form of adultery or old age. One key to apprehending her protagonists is the ironic contrast between what Brookner (and we) know and perceive, and their own often limited, naive, tragi-comic struggles. These women have to learn, through their suffering female self, that emotional fulfilment is often frustrated by intellectual achievement.

The creator is most in control in her latest novel *Family and Friends* (1985). Brookner uses a wedding photograph to distance herself and shows us the family with the eyes of an art historian: 'Sofka stands straight and stern, her shoulders braced, her head erect in the manner of two generations earlier' (p. 7). This saga is based on her own family, seen through art; through style which can vivify the appearance but reify the personality.

Sofka is the widow of a rich industrialist who came to England early this century. Through the two contrasting sons and daughters we are presented with two opposing attitudes to life, exemplified in the quotation from Goethe; 'he who lets himself be moulded by law, order and prosperity will never become an intolerable neighbour. On the other hand rules and regulations ruin our true appreciation of nature and our powers to express it.' The repressive effect of the interiorisation of rules is harrowingly contrasted with self-seeking hedonism, which allows a short-lived gaiety, ending in superficiality.

Brookner's form is clear, with one brief chapter dedicated to each character in turn. Fifty years of their lives are encompassed in 180 pages, a paradigm of conciseness. Some critics admire this elegant brevity, others deplore the exclusion of the wider world, the second world war. However, Brookner knows her limits, the war would detract from her main concern with the life not lived, the risks not taken. It is the narrator who takes risks, representing fifty years, her longest time-span and largest cast so far.

This is a family saga, but excluding much enumeration of events. A. N. Wilson considers

> the brilliance with which she solves the chronicle problem makes this book memorable. Brookner has chosen the medium of photography to help her and the artifice works very well. This is because so many of us hold together in our minds our own familiar mythologies by the perusal of photograph albums that we do not recognise it as an artifice.[24]

The role of art historian allows Brookner to observe her characters mould themselves into styles. Betty looks like Colette; her frustrations, caused by wanting too much, are only glimpsed from the outside. Her brother Frederick 'dashing, handsome' is selfish, sensuous, virtually a cliché. Brookner's purpose is to show how far some characters allow themselves to be stereotyped by society. These two are glamorous, greedy, finally empty. Contrasted to them are the two 'good' siblings who subordinate their desires to their mother's moral dictates and lose the capacity for enjoyment. Brookner has been compared to Henry James[25] in the portrayal of impulses not fulfilled, the stifling of instinct by reason and calm. As in many of his novels there is an underlying sense of sadness caused by stultifying over-civilisation. Her writing mirrors her themes by avoiding what it cannot cope with. This is a triumph of form over content, both in their lives and her style. Surface emotion glosses over reality, civilisation destroys itself, scarcely noticing Nazi Germany.

Her Jewish family combines worldliness with hypersensitivity to anxiety and pain. The matriarch's stifling of her offspring is represented with mercilessly understated irony. Sorrows are not as desperate as in early nineteenth-century romantic novels, but claustrophobic, quietly soul-destroying. The family offers security, but the price is the destruction of creativity. The psychological intensity of this immigrant family prevents escape by the suppressing of desires.

This is a novel about appearances, a fact bewailed by some critics.[26] It also investigates self-deception, hypocrisy and duplicity. 'Harm may be done but it is never meant' is the chilling judgement on the calculating Sofka, who allows one son to be overburdened by the family business, the other to become a feckless, kept man. Like Compton-Burnett, Brookner posits family as manipulating excessive power. Both these women novelists, in controlled, precise, almost stagey prose, accept the wretchedness of the human condition, the destructiveness of the family bond.

Brookner represents the implications of the life not lived. The whole parasitic family is living off the factory, to which is dedicated the emotional potential of two men, who, sheep-like, accept the burden of duty, which here reifies the self. It might be objected that the moral and emotional dilemmas of Alfred are underdeveloped, as is his life. However Brookner ends brilliantly, looking at a family photograph with Alfred beside his favourite cousin Nettie. 'Wait for the dancing to begin.' This final sentence leaves work for our imagination, inviting the reader in.

Family and Friends was inspired by a photograph of her own family, shown her at a gathering of distant relatives.

> I knew nothing of these people and was obliged to invent them. But somewhere in the course of this invention I discovered that I was writing what amounted to a true chronicle. Whether this was an obscure form of unconscious memory, whether it was intuition or the exhilaration of disposing of these characters whom I had always seen as immensely powerful, I have no idea. . .It laid many ghosts; it was the game aspect which intrigued me.[27]

(Murdoch calls fabulation 'games-playing'.)

Her female characters are often presented as static images, created by clothes, hairstyles and environment. 'It is the duty of girls to marry happily' (p. 13), states the matriarch, unaware of the contradiction. 'Out of the debris of a European family, Sofka has bred an English aristocrat' (p. 22). The woman creates where she can, exploiting the only power she has – that over her children's upbringing. She passes on to her girls the restrictive knowledge that 'a woman of 35 is to be pitied, and is indeed pitied by those who ignore her essence and who will most certainly denigrate her virtues' (p. 125). Betty concentrates on self-creation, making a work of art out of her appearance 'like a painting by Foujita'. Whereas the rejected 'Mimi believes hearts are won by honesty, not believing for a moment that Betty's is the surer way' (p. 56). Mimi is modelled on Brookner's own mother, for whom she feels immense compassion for having to stay at home. Mimi's profound despair proceeds from a sense of exclusion from the living world. 'It is not Frank for whom she yearns, but for the missing factor in herself that would have brought Frank to her side. She blames herself entirely for this omission, and maybe she is right. . .It is as much as she can do now to avoid pain, simply to avoid pain' (p. 126).

BROOKNER'S LANGUAGE

The simplicity of that sentence could be called postmodernist. Brookner favours directness to represent a sad, interiorised vision of women who are losers in love. Her rhythms aptly echo the depressions of her outsiders, with their romantic inability to compromise, their preferring of loneliness to the second rate.

Her writing has been praised for its subtlety and clarity. It can descend to obviousness and occasional banality. But it is redeemed by insights into her protagonists, such as 'to suppose that those who are sexually inactive are also sexually inarticulate is a grave mistake, but one that is made with disheartening frequency' (Family and Friends, pp. 116–17). Her writing is less insightful about the sexually attractive whom she views not as manipulated but as making 'a cult of themselves. . .dishonourable, terrifying'. This is virtually a male, exterior standpoint. However, she scores in showing when roles take over, turning people into stereotypes.

'I mean to be amusing rather than critical,' she insisted in a television interview.[28] Delightful aphorisms support her claim, such as 'It is not true that Satan finds work for idle hands; that is just what he doesn't' (Hotel du Lac, p. 158). However it is in evocation of mood that she is most skilful, in a late eighteenth-century way. 'The empty lake, the fitful light, the dream-like slowness seemed to have an allegorical significance' (Hotel du Lac, p. 159). At times she communicates an almost physical sense of sight, smell and texture, as when Frederick, in Family and Friends, wanders sensually round the market at Nice.

> The sharp and almost sickening smell of the cheeses laid out on leaves
> of fern and palm, the sudden gleam of a coffee machine and the spurt
> of its steam, the blessed sight of the fresh loaves of bread, freshly baked
> for lunchtime, being set up vertically in the window of a baker's shop.
> (p. 145)

She excels at the representation of distress: 'It was the very
coldness of her common sense that afflicted her with almost
senile terror' (*Hotel du Lac*, p. 166). She foregrounds an
incapacity to accept onself. 'I have held this rather dim and
trusting personality together for a considerable length of time
and though I have certainly bored others, I was not allowed
to bore myself' (ibid., p. 9).

Her consciousness cuts down images to the minimum; of
the hotel we are told merely of its veal-coloured carpets and
curtains, symbolising its deadening tranquillity. She has been
praised as French in her brevity. Certainly her six books are
more like continental novellas in length – long short stories.
The concentration on the psychological tension caused by an
unrequited affection recalls *Corrine* by Mme de Staël (1807)
and *Adolphe* by her lover Benjamin Constant.

Brookner's preference for 'realistic' writing might be
considered insular. Here it helps make sense of personal
experience. Indeed the demands of many readers for social
and psychological realism can only be met by incorporating
such personal experience. Her language humanises what it
touches, making the 'lineaments of unsatisfied desire' bear-
able. In exposing herself she has reflected 'the fate of so
many more among my fellow mortals', as George Eliot
claimed of *Adam Bede* in 1859.

CONCLUSION

Brookner's fictions reveal the effect of unconscious images of
self on conscious behaviour. She told Hermione Lee that 'the
novel speaks of states of mind which forced me to do
something about these states of mind.'[29] One of the stimulating
aspects of her writing is that the protagonists are often experts

on the interpreting of invention: Ruth Weiss on the invention
of women in Balzac, Edith Hope on romantic myths. In a
concealed but subversive way these heroines, apparently
helpless, control their world and gain a brief authority. Ruth's
saga is uninteresting to her colleagues until it is made into a
fiction – as happened to Brookner herself. Brookner is asking
implicitly if fiction reflects the world or reinvents it.

Brookner states, 'in a curious way only fiction-writers are
telling the truth.'[30] Yet she sees how often the unconscious
chooses fictional images which damage the truth. There is a
potential contradiction here, in her heroines: they represent
the harrowing discrepancy between what the intelligent
modern woman can see rationally and her retrogressive
emotional attitudes. 'One has to use one's own life; one has
no other material. These novels are a transcript from a
random, rather unsuccessful passage through life.'[31] She uses
her self, like many women, but not just for therapy, rather
for scrutiny, in order to break through to a clearer vision:

> Romanticism is not just a mode, it literally enters into every life.
> Women will never get rid of just waiting for the right man. In certain
> situtations reason doesn't work and that's the most desolating discovery
> of all. Edith Hope is neither a feminist nor a complacent consumer of
> men. She would like the ideal: romance to end in domesticity. Romantic
> hopefulness is constant in spite of the sense of defeat. *Hotel du Lac* is
> meant to be a love story. . .about the ideal of love.[32]

Brookner admits she finds both her heroines and herself
exasperating, damaged by having unrealistic goals, incompat-
ible with the conduct of life. Her self-revealing honesty in
interviews allows us to see how she uses her own emotions,
her own frustrations to decode old fictions and examine how
far they still keep us in thrall.

Paul Bailey nevertheless maintains that 'a certain dimension
is lacking, especially in the peripheral characters'.[33] The men
are frequently shadowy, reflections of what the heroines want
or how they are disappointed. In the first and last novels
Brookner represents a group, both what they feel they are
and what they wish to be 'which is the story of most of us'.[34]
She is feminist in viewing her protagonists' nineteenth-
century predicaments with twentieth-century awareness. She

keeps closely to the structure of romantic fiction ('form will save us'), seldom satirising, because the protagonist already knows the opposite happens in life. She will fail to reach out, exploit her sensibility, her talent, because she still conceives of herself in relation to men. Brookner investigates how limits imposed by convention gradually become part of our make-up. She writes from the inside about failures of nerve which eventually atrophy the individual. A Marxist might point out that she illustrates the breaking-down of the liberal ideology of the individual, now doomed to a solipsistic existence; lack of commitment leaves us bereft.

Women's novels were relegated until recently to a sub-culture, the domain of women, teaching women how others feel and behave. It is mainly the feminist publishing houses and feminist literary critics who have redeemed this vast category from subculture to mainstream. Feminist literary critics, from Showalter to Spender, have uncovered rich layers of signification and ideology. From the early eighteenth century to Brookner the women's novel represents what is problematic in the relations between the public and the private sphere. They show how men control, like Maurice in Brookner's *Providence*, while offering the readers clues not apparent to the heroine. The protagonists frequently do not know how to behave, how to react, repressed by their background, longing for what patriarchy promises, but seldom gives. They attempt to conform to cultural conventions, hoping to fulfil themselves emotionally and intellectually through one masterful male – who seldom falls for the repressed heroine. Brookner dramatises the double-bind, the unfairness of the contradictory aims presented to women.

The 'woman's novel' raises the question of how far one can speak of a 'woman's language'. This is widely debated and has given rise to three theoretical stances: First are those who consider the differing speech of the two sexes as a function of their differing roles; secondly, those who foreground the powerlessness of women, viewing it not as expressing a specifically female identity, but as sharing aspects of any subordinate group. Finally, many theorists, especially the French, believe that langauge is related to gender identity through our connection with the body and sexual desire.

(Writers like Murdoch would dismiss the distinction.)[35]

Discussion of language leads to a discussion of texts. French feminists would not uphold the rigid English distinction. Their ideas throw imaginative light on Brookner's practice. Cixous states that 'woman physically materialises what she's thinking, she signifies it with her body'[36] like so many romantic heroines. Cixous claims that women are all in the Realm of the Gift in that they are generous in giving themselves; Brookner's protagonists wish to give the whole of themselves to a (non-existent) male. Thus writing and plot form part of an inextricable whole. Certainly Brookner conflates 'feminine' and 'female', seeing the social construct, the feminine imposed by cultural norms, as identical with the biological.

American literary critics consider that women's writing includes both the author's self-image and an implicit critique of patriarchal society. Gilbert and Gubar postulate a real woman in the text (which Brookner admits) and stress the resulting imagery of disease and health, fragmentation and wholeness. They accept the authoress as transcendental source and meaning of her text, without looking for the silences and contradictions. Why is Brookner silent about feminist revaluation of women's potential, though she knows of it? Why does she state the greedy are happier, yet always represent sensual, grasping women ending as miserably as the repressed? Brookner may be called post-feminist in that she observes the constraints on women, yet cannot reject them as a feminist would, because she *feels* their continuing hold on the female conscious and unconscious.

NOTES

1. Dale Spender, *Mothers of the Novel* (Pandora, 1986). Marilyn Butler gave an incisive critique of Spender's approach on Radio 3, May 1986.
2. Nancy K. Miller, 'Plots and plausibilities in women's fiction', in E. Showalter (ed.), *The New Feminist Criticism* (Virago, 1986).
3. Spender, op. cit.
4. For more on this topic see Walter Ong, *Orality and Literacy* (Methuen, 1983).
5. Aphra Behn's plays are lively, bawdy critiques of Restoration attitudes. She wrote the first novels in English: *Orinooko* and *Love-letters between a Nobleman and his Sister* (1687; Virago 1987), an incisive study of

physical and mental breakdown. Behn provides another example of a woman whose work was unjustly neglected until recently.

6. See Spender, op. cit.
7. Gillian Beer, *Romance* (Methuen, 1970), makes skilful use of recent criticism.
8. Rosalind Coward, 'Are women's novels feminist novels?', *Feminist Review*, 5 (1980), develops a useful analysis of this topic.
9. Myra Jehlen, 'Archimedes and the paradox of feminist criticism', in Keohane et al. (eds), *Feminist Theory* (Harvester Press, 1982), pp. 189–215.
10. Ibid.
11. Interview with John Haffenden, *The Literary Review*, September 1984, pp. 25–30.
12. Elizabeth Bowen, *The Death of the Heart* (Penguin, 1962).
13. See Eva Figes, *Sex and Subterfuge* (Macmillan, 1982).
15. Philip Larkin in his now famous re-evaluation of Barbara Pym, in *The Times Literary Supplement*, 20 January 1977.
15. *Rhine Journey* (Macmillan, 1980), displays power, conciseness, shrewdness and delicacy.
16. In an interview, October 1985.
17. *Times Literary Supplement*, 20 January 1977.
18. See note 11 above.
19. Interview with Hermione Lee, Channel 4, September 1985.
20. See note 11 above.
21. See note 19 above.
22. Interview with Richard Mayne, Kaleidoscope, Radio 4, October 1984.
23. Marina Vaizey, Critics Forum, Radio 3, 3 November 1984.
24. *Times Literary Supplement*, 6 September 1985, p. 973.
25. Critics Forum, Radio 3, September 1985.
26. Paul Bailey, Critics Forum, Radio 3, September 1985.
27. Talk on Radio 3, printed in *Extra*, no. 1 (1985).
28. See note 15 above.
29. Ibid.
30. See note 11 above.
31. Ibid.
32. Ibid.
33. See note 26 above.,
34. See note 23 above.
35. For more on this topic see E. Abel (ed.), *Writing and Sexual Difference* (Harvester Press, 1970; Moira Monteith (ed.), *Women's Writing: a Challenge to Theory* (Harvester Press, 1986); and D. Cameron, *Feminism and Linguistic Theory* (Methuen, 1985).
36. *New French Feminisms* (Harvester Press, 1981), pp. 245–64.

Glossary

Anima – the feminine principle in all of us, as defined by Jung.

Biologism – a tendency to explain by reducing to biological causes.

Deconstruction – a radical critique of western thinking, initiated by Derrida, because meaning and truth were too fixed in time (and space). He considers deconstruction a 'strategy within philosophy' to displace philosophic hierarchies and closures. One of his strategies is to deconstruct concepts in western thought based on oppositions such as dark–light, active–passive, male–female, mad–sane, which exclude the sharing of these attributes. Deconstructing such polarities opens them to new meanings and allows us to explore and redefine maleness, madness etc.

Discourse – a stretch of language longer than a sentence (in linguistics). A type of language which needs to be understood in relation to its own conventions, such as a church service, a politburo pronouncement or a TV chat show. We are already modifying patriarchal discourse by saying 'human being' instead of the exclusive 'man', etc.

Fabulation – concern with fantasy and form in fiction, ideas and ideals rather than things. See Robert Scholes, *Fabulation* (1967).

Gender – aspects which are changeable; socially constructed male–femaleness as opposed to biological male–femaleness which is called *Sex*.

Ideology – the sum of ways we both live and represent to ourselves our relationship to conditions of existence. Ideology is inscribed in discourses, myths, presentations of 'how things are'. It offers only partial, selective, sometimes contradictory knowledge. Because it is a characteristic of language to be overlooked, the differences it constructs may seem to be natural, universal and unchangeable,

166

whereas they are produced by a specific form of social organisation – which can be modified. Literature represents the myths and imaginary versions of real social relationships which constitute ideology. The innovative thinking is Althusser's: 'What is represented in ideology is not the system of real relations which govern the existence of individuals, but the *imaginary*'.

Impressionism – conveys the author's state of mind, impression or mood rather than external or objective descriptions (as in Virginia Woolf).

Intertextuality – the reader's experience of other texts. Intertextual elements are the recognition of similarities and differences between text and all other texts we have read. Most novels are intertextual constructs, products of various cultural discourses on which the writing relies for intelligibility and thus needs reader as interpreter.

Langue – Saussure's term for written language that makes possible our speech acts (*parole*).

Modernism – international reaction in fiction, poetry, drama and music against realism. It stresses the aesthetic, formal, mythic and symbolist. In the English novel it denotes writers like Joyce and Woolf, less interested in detailed description than in states of mind, experiments with language and fragmentation of form.

Naturalism – Novel-writing based on extensive research into social conditions and their effect on the individual. The leading exponent is Zola, influenced by Darwin's evolutionary explanation of life.

Nouveau Roman – French novel concentrating on exploration of the world of objects rather than 'character', as in Robbe-Grillet's *La Jalousie*.

Omniscient Narrator – author who narrates as if s/he knows everything about the characters, as in some nineteenth-century novels.

Poststructuralism – developments in philosophy and criticism since Barthes. The technique used is termed deconstruction.

Reification – treating person or idea as a thing.

Semiology – science of signs based on the work of the linguist Saussure. As developed by Lacan it is useful in film and literary criticism.

Sign – unit of language consisting of a signifier (often a word) and a signified (idea) linked arbitrarily, not necessarily together.

Stereotype – oversimplified mental representation of category of person.

Structuralism – Analysis and understanding of culture as a system of signs, of which language is often used as a model. Systematic inventories of elements and their possibilities to account for meaning in literature.

Bibliographies of Individual Novelists

A. S. BYATT

Novels

Shadow of a Sun (London, Chatto & Windus, 1964; New York, Harcourt Brace, 1964)

The Game (London, Chatto & Windus, 1967; New York, Scribner, 1968)

The Virgin in the Garden (London, Chatto & Windus, 1978; New York, Knopf, 1979)

Still Life (London, Chatto & Windus, 1985)

Sugar (Short stories) (London, Chatto & Windus, 1987)

Other

Degrees of Freedom: The Novels of Iris Murdoch (London, Chatto & Windus, 1965; New York, Barnes & Noble, 1965)

Wordsworth and Coleridge in Their Time (London, Nelson, 1970; New York, Crane Russak, 1973)

Iris Murdoch (London, Longman, 1976)

Editor, *The Mill on the Floss* by George Eliot (London, Penguin, 1979)

ANITA BROOKNER

Jacques-Louis David (London, Chatto & Windus, 1980)

A Start in Life (London, Jonathan Cape, 1981)

Providence (London, Jonathan Cape, 1982)

Look at Me (London, Jonathan Cape, 1983)

Hotel du Lac (London, Jonathan Cape, 1984)

Family and Friends (London, Jonathan Cape, 1985)

A Misalliance (London, Jonathan Cape, 1986)

A Friend from England (London, Jonathan Cape, 1987)

MARGARET DRABBLE

Novels
A Summer Bird-Cage (London, Weidenfeld and Nicolson, 1963; New York, Morrow, 1964)
The Garrick Year (London, Weidenfeld and Nicolson, 1964; New York, Morrow, 1965)
The Millstone (London, Weidenfeld and Nicolson, 1965; New York, Morrow, 1966; as *Thank You All Very Much*, New York, New American Library, 1969)
Jerusalem the Golden (London, Weidenfeld and Nicolson; New York, Morrow, 1967)
The Waterfall (London, Weidenfeld and Nicolson; New York, Knopf, 1969)
The Needle's Eye (London, Weidenfeld and Nicolson; New York, Knopf, 1972)
The Realms of Gold (London, Weidenfeld and Nicolson; New York, Knopf, 1975)
The Ice Age (London, Weidenfeld and Nicolson; New York, Knopf, 1977).
The Middle Ground (London, Weidenfeld and Nicolson; New York, Knopf, 1980.
The Radiant Way (London, Weidenfeld and Nicolson, 1987)

Short Stories
Penguin Modern Stories 3, with others (London, Penguin, 1969)

Uncollected Short Stories
'Hassan's Tower', in *Winter's Tales 12*, ed. A. D. Maclean, (London, Macmillan; New York, St Martin's Press, 1966)
'A Voyage to Cytherea', in *Mademoiselle* (New York), December 1967.
'The Reunion', in *Winter's Tales 14*, ed. Kevin Crossley-Holland (London, Macmillan; New York, St. Martin's Press, 1968)
'The Gifts of War', in *Winter's Tales 16*, ed. A. D. Maclean (London, Macmillan, 1970; New York, St. Martin's Press, 1971)
'Crossing the Alps', in *Mademoiselle* (New York), February 1971
'A Successful Story', in *Spare Rib* (London), 1973
'A Day in the Life of a Smiling Woman', in *In the Looking Glass*. eds Nancy Dean and Myra Stark (New York, Putnam, 1977)

Plays
Bird of Paradise (produced London, 1969).
Screenplays: *Isadora*, with Melvyn Bragg and Clive Exton, 1969;
 A Touch of Love, 1969.
Television Play: *Laura*, 1964.

Other
Wordsworth (London, Evans, 1966: New York, Arco, 1969)
Arnold Bennett: A Biography (London, Weidenfeld and Nicolson;
 New York, Knopf, 1974)
For Queen and Country: Britain in the Victorian Age (juvenile).
 (London, Deutsch, 1978; New York, Seabury Press, 1979).
A Writer's Britain: Landscape in Literature (London, Thames and
 Hudson; New York, Knopf, 1979)
Virginia Woolf: A Personal Debt (New York, Aloe, 1973)
Editor, with B. S. Johnson, *London Consequences* (a group novel).
 (London, Greater London Arts Association, 1972)
Editor, *Lady Susan, The Watsons, Sanditon*, by Jane Austen,
 (London, Penguin, 1974)
Editor, *The Genius of Thomas Hardy* (London, Weidenfeld and
 Nicolson; New York, Knopf, 1976)
Editor, with Charles Osborne, *New Stories 1* (London, Arts Council,
 1976)
Manuscript Collections: Boston University; University of Tulsa,
 Oklahoma.
Critical Studies: *Margaret Drabble: Puritanism and Permissiveness* by
 Valerie Grosvenor Myer (London, Vision Press, 1974); *The
 Novels of Margaret Drabble: Equivocal Figures* by Ellen Cronan
 Rose (London, Macmillan, 1980)

EVA FIGES

Novels
Equinox (London, Secker and Warburg, 1966)
Winter Journey (London, Faber, 1967; New York, Hill and
 Wang, 1968)
Konek Landing (London, Faber, 1969)
B. (London, Faber, 1972)
Days (London, Faber, 1974)
Nelly's Version (London, Secker and Warburg, 1977)
Waking (London, Hamish Hamilton, 1981)
Light (London, Hamish Hamilton, 1983)
The Seven Ages (London, Hamish Hamilton, 1986)

Radio Plays
Time Regained (1980); *Days*, from her own novel.

Other
The Musicians of Bremen: Retold (juvenile) (London, Blackie, 1967)
The Banger (juvenile) (London, Deutsch; New York, Lion Press, 1968)
Patriarchal Attitudes: Women in Society (London, Faber; New York, Stein and Day, 1970)
Scribble Sam (juvenile) (London, Deutsch; New York, McKay, 1971)
Tragedy and Social Evolution (London, Calder; New York, Riverrun Press, 1976)
Little Eden: A Child at War (autobiography) (London, Faber, 1978)
Sex and Subterfuge (Macmillan, 1982)
Editor, *Classic Choice 1* (London, Blackie, 1965)
Editor, *Modern Choice 1 and 2* (London, Blackie, 2 vols, 1965–66)
Editor, with Abigail Mozley and Dinah Livingstone, *Women Their World* (Gisburn, Lancashire, Platform Poets, 1980)
Translator, *The Gadarene Club*, by Martin Walser (London, Longman, 1960)
Translator, *The Old Car*, by Elisabeth Borchers (London, Blackie, 1967)
Translator, *He and I and the Elephants*, by Bernhard Grzimek (London, Deutsch-Thames and Hudson; New York, Hill and Wang, 1967)
Translator, *Little Fadette*, by George Sand (London, Blackie, 1967)
Translator, *A Family Failure*, by Renate Rasp (London, Calder and Boyars, 1970)
Translator, *The Deathbringer*, by Manfred von Conta (London, Calder and Boyars, 1971)

IRIS MURDOCH

Under the Net (London, Chatto and Windus; New York, Viking Press, 1954)
The Flight from the Enchanter (London, Chatto and Windus; New York, Viking Press, 1956)
The Sandcastle (London, Chatto and Windus; New York, Viking Press, 1957)
The Bell (London, Chatto and Windus; New York, Viking Press, 1958)

A Severed Head (London, Chatto and Windus; New York, Viking Press, 1961)

An Unofficial Rose (London, Chatto and Windus; New York, Viking Press, 1962)

The Unicorn (London, Chatto and Windus; New York, Viking Press, 1963)

The Italian Girl (London, Chatto and Windus; New York, Viking Press, 1964)

The Red and the Green (London, Chatto and Windus; New York, Viking Press, 1965)

The Time of the Angels (London, Chatto and Windus; New York, Viking Press, 1966)

The Nice and the Good (London, Chatto and Windus; New York, Viking Press, 1968)

Bruno's Dream (London, Chatto and Windus; New York, Viking Press, 1969)

A Fairly Honourable Defeat (London, Chatto and Windus; New York, Viking Press, 1970)

An Accidental Man (London, Chatto and Windus, 1971; New York, Viking Press, 1972)

The Black Prince (London, Chatto and Windus; New York, Viking Press, 1973)

The Sacred and Profane Love Machine (London, Chatto and Windus; New York, Viking Press, 1974)

A Word Child (London, Chatto and Windus; New York, Viking Press, 1975)

Henry and Cato (London, Chatto and Windus; 1976, New York, Viking Press, 1977)

The Sea, The Sea (London, Chatto and Windus; New York, Viking Press, 1978)

Nuns and Soldiers (London, Chatto and Windus, 1980; New York, Viking Press, 1981)

The Philosopher's Pupil (London, Chatto and Windus; New York, Viking Press, 1982)

The Good Apprentice (London, Chatto and Windus; New York, Viking Press, 1985)

Plays

A Severed Head, with J. B. Priestley, adaptation of the novel by Murdoch (produced Bristol and London, 1963; New York, 1964) (London, Chatto and Windus, 1964)

The Italian Girl, with James Saunders, adaptation of the novel by

Murdoch (produced Bristol, 1967; London, 1968) (London, French, 1969)

The Servants and the Snow (produced London, 1970). Included in *The Three Arrows and The Servants and the Snow* (1973)

The Three Arrows (produced Cambridge, 1972). Included in *The Three Arrows and The Servants in the Snow* (1973)

The Three Arrows, and The Servants and the Snow: Two Plays (London, Chatto and Windus, 1973; New York, Viking Press, 1974)

Art and Eros (produced London, 1980)

Verse
A Year of Birds (Tisbury, Wiltshire, Compton Press, 1978)

Other
Sartre, Romantic Rationalist (Cambridge, Bowes; New Haven, Connecticut, Yale University Press, 1953)

The Sovereignty of Good over Other Concepts (lecture) (Cambridge, University Press, 1967)

The Sovereignty of Good (essays) (London, Routledge, 1970; New York, Schocken, 1971)

The Fire and the Sun: Why Plato Banished the Artists (London and New York, Oxford University Press, 1977)

Acastos: Two Platonic Dialogues (London, Chatto, 1985)

FAY WELDON

Novels
The Fat Woman's Joke (London, MacGibbon and Kee, 1967: as *. . .and the Wife Ran Away*, New York, McKay, 1968)

Down among the Women (London, Heinemann, 1971; New York, St. Martin's Press, 1972)

Female Friends (London, Heinemann; New York, St Martin's Press, 1975)

Remember Me (London, Hodder and Stoughton; New York, Random House, 1976)

Words of Advice (New York, Random House, 1977; as *Little Sisters*, London, Hodder and Stoughton, 1978)

Praxis (London, Hodder and Stoughton; New York, Summit, 1978)

Puffball (London, Hodder and Stoughton; New York, Summit, 1980)

The President's Child (London, Hodder and Stoughton; New York, Summit, 1982)

Little Sisters (London, Hodder and Stoughton; New York, Summit, 1984)

The Life and Loves of a She-Devil (London, Hodder and Stoughton; New York, Summit, 1984)

The Shrapnel Academy (London, Hodder and Stoughton, 1986)

The Heart of the Country (London, Hutchinson, 1987)

Short Stories

Watching Me, Watching You (London, Hodder and Stoughton, 1981)

Plays

Permanence, in *Mixed Blessings* (produced London, 1969) (London, Methuen, 1970)

Time Hurries On, in *Scene Scripts*, ed. Michael Marland (London, Longman, 1972)

Words of Advice (produced London, 1974) (London, French, 1974)

Moving House (produced Farnham, Surrey, 1976)

Friends (produced Guildford, 1978)

Mr. Director (produced Richmond, 1978)

Polaris (broadcast, 1978). Published in *Best Radio Plays of 1978: The Giles Cooper Award Winners* (London, Eyre, Methuen, 1979)

Action Replay (produced Birmingham, 1978) (London, French, 1980)

Radio Plays: *Spider*, 1972; *Mr. Fox and Mr. First*, 1974; *Housebreaker*, 1974; *The Doctor's Wife*, 1975; *Polaris*, 1978; *All the Bells of Paradise*, 1979; *Weekend*, 1979.

Television Plays: *Wife in a Blond Wig*, 1966; *The Fat Woman's Tale*, 1966; *What About Me*, 1967; *Dr. De Waldon's Therapy*, 1967; *Goodnight Mrs. Dill*, 1967; *The 45th Unmarried Mother*, 1967; *Fall of the Goat*, 1967; *Ruined Houses*, 1968; *Venus Rising*, 1968; *The Three Wives of Felix Hull*, 1968; *Hippy Hippy Who Cares*, 1968; *£13083*, 1968; *The Loophole*, 1969; *Smokescreen*, 1969; *Poor Mother*, 1970; *Office Party*, 1971; *On Trial* (Upstairs, Downstairs series), 1971; *Old Man's Hat*, 1972; *A Splinter of Ice*, 1972; *Hands*, 1972; *The Lament of an Unmarried Father*, 1972, *A Nice Rest*, 1972; *Comfortable Words*, 1973; *Desirous of Change*, 1973; *In Memoriam*, 1974; *Poor Baby*, 1975; *The Tale of Timothy Bagshott*, 1975; *Aunt Tatty*, from the story by Elizabeth Bowen, 1975; *Act of Rape*, 1977; *Married Love*, 1977; *Act of Hypocrisy* (*Jubilee* series), 1977; *Chickabiddy* (*Send in the Girls* series), 1978; *Pride and Prejudice*, from the novel by Jane Austen, 1980; *Honey Ann*, 1980; *Life for Christine*, 1980; *Watching Me, Watching You* (*Leap in the Dark* series), 1980.

Other
Editor, with Elaine Feinstein, *New Stories 4* (London, Hutchinson, 1979)
Letters to Alice on First Reading Jane Austen (London, Coronet, 1985)

Bibliography

All books are published in London, unless otherwise indicated.
All Harvester books are published in Sussex.

USEFUL GENERAL CRITICISM

M. Bradbury (ed.), *Possibilities: Essays on the State of the Novel* (Oxford University Press, 1973). *The Novel Today* 1977 Fontana. This contains Murdoch, 'Against Dryness' and Lodge, 'The Novelist at the Crossroads', 1979). *The Contemporary English Novel* (Arnold, 1979). This includes Byatt, 'People in Paper Houses', and Lorna Sage, 'Female Fictions'.

A. Burgess, *The Novel Now* (Faber, 1967). Burgess is wide-ranging and idiosyncratic, with a perceptive chapter on women.

D. J. Enright, *A Mania for Words* (Chatto, 1984). Enright takes a traditional approach. He includes a short article on the female *The Tale of Genji*.

B. Hardy, *The Appropriate Form* (Athlone, 1964); *Tellers and Listeners* (Athlone, 1975) Perceptive writing from a woman critic (was Leavisite).

R. Jackson, *Fantasy: The Literature of Subversion* (Methuen, 1983). She uses new criticism incisively.

G. Josipovici, *The World and the Book* (Macmillan, 1971). Josipovici introduces French criticism (especially Barthes), imaginatively; with essays on Proust, Dante and the rise of the novel.

D. Lodge, *The Language of Fiction*. Readable modern criticism. *Working with Structuralism* (Routledge and Kegan Paul, 1981). Lodge does not provide a thorough introduction, but he approaches the topic for a beginner.

W. Ong, *Orality and Literacy* (Methuen, 1982). Ong provides an imaginative erudite study of the oral traditions of the working-class and women.

C. Rawling (ed.), *Popular Fiction and Social Change*, contains a seminal article on science fiction by M. Jordin.

J.-P. Sartre, *What is Literature?* (Harper-Colophon, New York, 1965). Worth re-reading.

T. Tanner, *City of Words: American Fiction 1950–70* (Cape, 1971). Tanner states that 'a novel should be able to contain in language our destiny'.

A. Wilson, *Diversity and Depth* (1984). Angus Wilson has collected a range of brief reviews, on *Clarissa*, Camus, Murdoch, Claude Simon and many others.

A useful reference work is *Contemporary Novelists* (St Martins Press, 1982). It offers brief accounts of the novels and bibliographies.

CONTEMPORARY CRITICISM

Belsey, Catherine, *Critical Practice* (Methuen, 1980). This text provides the best written brief introduction to theories of Barthes and Derrida.

Barthes, Roland, *Mythologies* (Cape, 1972). These fascinating, concise, approachable essays use his sign-system to analyse myths, books, even wrestling. Read *S/Z* (Cape, 1975) for his analysis of Balzac's realism.

A Barthes Reader ed. Susan Sontag (Cape, 1985) provides a brilliant, idiosyncratic introduction, putting him in an older French tradition.

Culler, Jonathan, *On Deconstruction: Theory and Criticism after Structuralism* (Cornell University Press, 1982). Culler is erudite and helpful.

Eagleton, Terry, *Myths of Power, a Marxist Study of the Brontës* (Macmillan, 1975) This offers a perceptive introduction to Marxist criticism. Then read his thorough *Marxism and Literary Theory* (Methuen, 1976). One of the most reliable introductions to recent theory is his paperback *Literary Theory* (Blackwell, 1983). Eagleton is a major contemporary critic.

Hawkes, Terence, *Structuralism and Semiotics* (Methuen, 1977). Hawkes offers an historical introduction, clear exposition and annotated bibliography.

Kearney, Richard, *The Wake of the Imagination: Ideas of Creativity in Western Culture* (Hutchinson, Winter 1987). This Irish philosopher writes on modern Frnech theory enthusiastically. He points out that postmodernism need not relinquish all humanism if it respects the ethical imagination.

Macherey, Pierre, *A Theory of Literary Production* (Routledge and Kegan Paul, 1978). This is a demanding text by a leading Marxist.

Punter, David, *The Hidden Script: Writing and the Unconscious* (Routledge, 1985). Punter offers an illuminating, uneven investigation of the unconscious in Carter, Lessing, Bainbridge, Ballard and others.

Further Reading

Bergonzi, Bernard, *The Myth of Modernism and Twentieth Century Literature* (Harvester Press, 1985). He relates literature to its cultural context.

Selden, Raman, *A Reader's Guide to Contemporary Literary Theory*. (Harvester Press, 1985). Professor Selden expounds theory from Bakhtin and Lukács to Foucault and Kristéva, with guides to further reading.

FEMINIST LITERARY CRITICISM

The most helpful introductions are:

Green and Kahn (eds), *Making a Difference* (Methuen, 1985). This collection includes essays on varieties of feminist criticism, American, French, black and lesbian criticism.

Humm, Maggie, *Feminist Criticism: Women as Contemporary Writers* (Harvester Press, 1986). Humm explores contemporary theory and its effect on women writers.

Moi, Toril, *Sexual/Textual Politics* (Methuen, 1985). Moi gives a clear, forceful theoretical underpinning which she claims feminist criticism needs.

Showalter, Elaine (ed.), *The New Feminist Criticism* (Virago, 1986). Professor Showalter includes many pathbreaking recent articles.

Re-reading Patriarchy

Figes, Eva, *Patriarchal Attitudes* (Macmillan, 1970) See chapter on Figes.

Greer, Germaine, *The Female Eunuch* (Paladin, 1970) Greer is still powerful.

Millett, Kate, *Sexual Politics* (Virago, 1970) Millett packs her punches. (The term patriarchy has been problematised in recent criticism.)

Reading/Writing like a Woman

These texts are listed chronologically, as there is a progress in the
approaches to 'Images of Women' in Anglo-American criticism.

Spacks, Patricia Meyer, *The Female Imagination* (New York, 1975).
Spacks bases her articles on perceptive discussions with students
about this vast and problematic topic. Today she is criticised for
revealing a white middle-class bias, but she is worth reading on
the nineteenth century.

Moers, Ellen, *Literary Women: The Great Writers* (New York,
Doubleday, 1976; Women's Press, 1978). Moers surveys nineteenth-century novelists brilliantly.

Showalter, Elaine, *A Literature of Their Own: British Women Novelists
from Brontë to Lessing* (Princeton University Press, 1977; Virago,
1978). Epoch making.

Fetterley, Judith. *The Resisting Reader: Feminist Approaches to
American Fiction* (Indiana University Press, 1978). This is a
valuable re-reading.

Gilbert, Sandra M. and Gubar, Susan, *The Madwoman in the Attic:
The Woman Writer and the Nineteenth Century Literary Imagination*
(Yale University Press, 1979). This is an exciting study which
does not exclude Jane Austen or George Eliot, though it
highlights implicit angers and frustrations.

Jacobus, Mary (ed.), *Women Writing and Writing about Women*
(Croom Helm, 1979).

Abel, Elizabeth (ed.), *Writing and Sexual Difference* (Harvester
Press, 1982). Abel includes some illuminating but demanding
theorists.

Deconstructing Gender

Keohane, Rosaldo and Gelpi, *Feminist Theory* (Harvester Press,
1982). These three editors introduce invaluable articles, including
Myra Jehlen, 'Archimedes and the Paradox of Feminist Criticism',
which opens 'Feminist thinking is really *rethinking*', pp. 189–940.

Marks, Elaine and de Courtivron, Isabelle (eds), *New French
Feminisms: An Anthology* (1980; Harvester Press, 1981). This
offers helpful translations from a wide selection of texts, difficult
to obtain elsewhere.

Jardine, Lisa, *Still Harping on Daughters: Women and Drama in the
Age of Shakespeare* (Harvester Press, 1983). Enlightening use of
feminist approaches.

Wandor, Michelene, *On Gender and Writing* (Pandora, 1983). This
book consists of useful interviews with a wide range of women
writers and feminists.

Kristéva, Julia, *Desire in Language: A Semiotic Approach to Literature and Art* (France, 1979; USA, 1980; Oxford, Blackwell, 1980). Difficult yet worthwhile.

Women Writing about Women Writing

Beauman, Nicola, *A Very Great Profession: The Women's Novel 1914–1939* (Virago, 1983). A superficial survey of the plots of many women's novels

Baym, Nina, *Women's Fiction* (Cornell, 1978). Baym's thesis is that pious heroines represent moral strength, and domesticity equals pragmatic feminism.

Ellmann, Mary, *Thinking about Women* (Virago, 1979).

Evans, Mari (ed.), *Black Women Writers 1950–1980* (New York, Anchor Press, 1984; Pluto Press, 1985). Evans represents a wonderful selection of interviews with major Black writers and articles on their work.

Figes, Eva, *Sex and Subterfuge* (Macmillan, 1982). Figes analyses similarities of structures in eighteenth-century English novelists, in a social context.

Hardwick, Elizabeth, *Seduction and Betrayal* (Weidenfeld and Nicolson, 1976). Hardwick's essays are readable, thought-provoking and delightfully brief.

Olsen, Tillie, *Silences* (1965–78; Virago, 1980). Tillie Olsen offers a poet's view of difficulties in writing and publishing.

Rich, Adrienne, *On Lies, Secrets and Silence: Selected Prose 1962–78* (1979; Virago, 1980). This is a major book by a leading lesbian.

Stubbs, Patricia, *Woman and Fiction: Feminism and the American Novel 1880–1920* (Harvester Press, 1979). This is an uneven but useful study.

Zeman, Anthea, *Presumptuous Girls: Women and Their World in the Serious Woman's Novel* (Weidenfeld and Nicolson, 1977). Zeman's title promises more than it gives, but covers interesting English novelists.

FEMINISM

Barrett, Michèle, *Women's Oppression Today* (Verso, 1980) provides a forceful introductory account.

Brunt, Rosalind and Rowan, Caroline, *Feminism, Culture and Politics* (Lawrence and Wishart, 1982). They present an exceedingly useful range of essays, including Barrett 'A Definition of Cultural Politics'.

Cameron, Deborah, *Feminism and Linguistic Theory* (Macmillan,

1985). The clearest comprehensive survey of the strengths (and weaknesses) of present theoretical positions, written with common sense and revolutionary vision.

Eisenstein, Hester, *Contemporary Feminist Thought* (Unwin Paperbacks, 1985). A wide-ranging account of differing historical, social and literary attitudes.

Heilbrun, Carolyn, *Toward a Recognition of Androgyny* (1973; New York, Harper-Colophon Books, 1974). This is a valuable analysis, and a necessary adjunct to feminist enquiry.

Miller, Casey and Swift, Kate, *Words and Women* (Pelican, 1979). They present a useful analysis of discrimination in the language of educational books.

Mitchell, Juliet, *Psychoanalysis and Feminism* (Penguin, 1976). Mitchell is one of the leading British feminists to use psychoanalysis.

Oakley, Ann, *Sex, Gender and Society* (M. T. Smith, 1972), offers helpful distinctions.

Spender, Dale, writes clearly and prolifically, but untheoretically. Her epochmaking book was *Man Made Language* (Routledge and Kegan Paul, 1980). Spender analyses patriarchal discrimination in everyday language, with many cogent examples. *Women of Ideas* (Ark Paperbacks, 1985) presents summaries of often neglected women writers and thinkers from Aphra Behn to the present day; *For the Record: The making and meaning of feminist knowledge* (The Women's Press, 1980). Spender offers accounts of ideas from Friedan onwards. *Mothers of the Novel* (Pandora, 1986), describes the lives of 100 women novelists before Jane Austen, but has too little analysis of their books.

Radcliffe Richards, Janet, *The Sceptical Feminist* (Penguin, 1983). This presents a sensible critique of a few exaggerated claims.

The Feminist Review contains many relevant articles. It is published three times a year by a collective, 65, Manor Rd, London N.16.

Three excellent women critics who use contemporary theory:

Beer, Gillian, *Romance* (Methuen, 1970). From the Middle Ages to the 1920s.

Fleenor, Juliann, E., *The Female Gothic* (Canada, Eden Press, 1983).

Jackson, Rosemary, *Fantasy: The Literature of Subversion* (Methuen, 1983).

Index